How to Love a Black Man when...

a sistah's guide to loving the brothers despite their flaws

By

sistahsophie

ISBN: 1461117747

ISBN-13: 978-1461117742

For my father and his son…

For my husband and our sons…

Love you guys

Table of contents

Introduction

And

Dedicated to My Brothers: An Awesome Wonder

Introduction

Greetings my sistahs, I bring you ancient peace and love. I wrote this book for us-all the real sistahs out there that never want to give up on our brothers-the Black Man.

For so long the Black Man has been beaten down by this society, deprived of life's freedoms, and stripped of his very manhood. His wealth and lands were plundered. His woman raped. His children bought and sold. The weight of the world has been on his shoulders with no tools to haul the load. The Black Man has been a slave; thrown in a cage; only half his story told.

Is it any wonder why the Black Man has such a difficult time relating to his woman? Is it any wonder why we have such a difficult time relating to him? Trying to love a Black Man can be a true test of even the strongest sistahs faith and endurance. It ain't easy loving the brothers. Lord knows it ain't easy. But I believe, and I know you do too, that ultimately they are worth it.

There is nothing more beautiful than the love between a Black Man and his Queen; nothing more beautiful than the Black Family. Black love binds, black love endures.

Together, I hope we can figure out how to love the Black Man despite it all, despite his flaws.

Peace and love.

Chapter 1

How to Love a Black Man when…He's a Mama's Boy

"Grown don't mean nothing to a mother. A child is a child. They get bigger, older, but grown? What's that suppose to mean? In my heart it don't mean a thing"-Toni Morrison

One of my children asked me the other day, "hey ma…do you think your life would be different if we (the children) weren't here?" I stopped to consider his question wondering if he meant would my life have been better or worse if I didn't have children. I'm pretty straight forward with my all my children whenever they ask a question; even the little ones. I never tell them some fat, white man will break into our house once a year to bring them presents; they know their parent's work hard to provide everything they have in life. I never tell them about fairies giving them money for their baby teeth or any of the other typical childhood fantasies parents tell their children. I just wasn't raised in that world. So I explained the simple truth about my journey as a mother by telling him:

"I was just a kid myself when I had you. The only thing I knew about life back then was life was hard. We were poor, your grandma was always in and out of rehab, and your uncle had been shipped 3,000 miles away to the only relatives we had willing to take him in. I had to get use to a lot of things children shouldn't have to get used to. I got use to never having enough to eat. Got use to Con-Ed shutting off the lights. Got use to moving from place to place. Too use to packing everything I owned in ten minutes so I could "vacate the premises". And very use to nothing but crazy every day. I bounced from one friends' couch to the other; slept on floors; and made myself cozy a few nights on a park bench. I didn't care about life. Didn't think too much about the future. I had nothing. I had no one. I was truly alone in this world.

I managed to graduate from high school and knew I had to come up with a way to feed myself. I applied for school but soon realized financial aid couldn't cover all my expenses. I filled out dozens of job applications but never got a call back. After repeatedly seeing a commercial to "be all that I could be" I decided to join the army reserves. I never thought of myself as a soldier, but the service guaranteed three hot meals, a warm bed, and eventually a job as one of Uncle Sam's G.I.s. Many young black people join for the same reasons. It's a way out of the hood. It was my only way out. So I took their exams, signed their forms, and was "good to go".

But the summer before I was set to leave I noticed that a lot of the girls from around my way, girls that were in the same position I was in- no family support, no job, etc. - still seemed to have everything they wanted in their lives: decked out apartments, designer shoes and clothes, new weaves, and money in their purses; with no conceivable way of affording all these things and no plans on joining the military anytime soon. I finally convinced one of them to let me in on the big secret and she confessed that it wasn't just the dope-boys she dated buying her all the stuff she had. She and many girls from the hood worked as dancers in strip clubs downtown.

"It was no big deal", my friend said. It was "easy" money.

"Better than hoe-ing on The Point (Hunt's Point in the Bronx)", she said, "Beats flipping burgers in some nasty, greasy uniform all day. All you have to do is take off your clothes and dance around for these tricks"

At the time I thought she was right. I thought about all the video girls on MTV and all the other women in the world that used their bodies to make money. It wasn't sex; it was just dancing; and my friend made it seem like it would be night after night of champagne and bubbles. I told her I would come by and check it out. See if I fit in. But the night she came to pick me up I was sick as a dog and had been vomiting all day. I never got sick like that and since my period was already a week late, I went to the Planned Parenthood the next morning only to find out I was pregnant with you. That news changed everything…changed my life.

Suddenly I was going to be somebody. Somebody's mother and responsible for a life greater than my own. I know now that your father wasn't mature enough to handle the situation (by the way, thanks for the sperm), but I welcomed the challenge with open arms. I prepared myself by getting a job and saving for my own place. I decided a career in nursing could provide for the both of us, so I went back to school while I was pregnant with you and later earned my degree. Since the day I became your mother, I've been working, going to school, and trying to be a good example for you guys. I love each and every one of you and couldn't imagine my life without you. So do I think my life would be different if you weren't here? Absolutely. I might have been a stripper!"

Of course he was shocked and embarrassed by my answer. He's 15. He's shocked and embarrassed by everything I do. But my kids know me; they know I give it to them straight. I went on to clarify that all those women using their bodies to make money don't have it easy as we might all think. They don't all do it for fun. They deal with a lot of shit to make that "easy" money. When the beauty fades and the tities sag, then what?

"So don't bring home any strippers!" I warned him, "I want a nice girl to give me grandchildren one day."

◊

The bond between mother and child is a special thing, a very special love. You love this little person before you can even see them. You carry them for almost a year. You bare excruciating pain to make sure they arrive safely into this world. Then once they are in your arms you never want to let them go. I'm amazed when I hear children from certain cultures say, "I hate my mother" or "my mom's a bitch". I'm even more disappointed to hear the children from my own culture follow suit, especially a son.

You can tell a lot about how a man will treat you based on his relationship with his mother. If he loves his mother, he will love you. If he is respectful to his mother, he will respect you. A man's mother may be the most perfect woman he knows. Or maybe they never got along and he has serious issues with all the women in his life.

What about his father? The presence of a man's father (or at least a father figure) can set an important example for him to be a good man; a good father and husband as well. His father could be a great! Maybe they still go fishing every Sunday like they did when he was a boy. Or maybe his father was a total deadbeat and never there for him. Either way it's important to know.

I have four sons and love then unconditionally. They know I'll always be "mom", always there for them when they need me. Do I think they're "mama's boys"? Yes, because they are boys now and I love every minute of it. The "mama's boys" I want to talk to you about are the grown ass men that still *act* like little boys when it comes to the relationship with their mothers. The real mama's boys.

◊

So what makes a man a mama's boy? Well, if a grown ass man still lives with his mama and she's still cooking for him, cleaning for him, and tucking him in at night…he's a mama's boy. Don't get me wrong. A lot of times in the black community parents live with their adult children out of necessity. That adult child now contributes to the household, but as an adult. They pay rent, buy food, and are responsible for keeping their part of the house clean. They come and go as they please but show respect for their parents by continuing to check in: "I'll be out late tonight Ma", etc. Even if a parent doesn't need help with household finances, an adult child may stay home while in college or grad school. Young women often stay home until they are married. Every family is different.

It's funny how human beings, the self-proclaimed superior species on the planet, make life more complicated than it has to be. Every lioness suckles her cub, teaches him how to hunt and how to survive. But once that cub makes his first kill, it's time to leave the pride. Every mother bird feeds her little hatchlings until they are strong enough to fly and leave the nest. It's the circle of life. It's nature. But some women, in their roles as mothers, are unable to let their sons grow up and become the men they need to be.

A friend of mine discovered she was dating a "mama's boy" after a year of confusion and heartache. The first red flag was that he was in his thirties and still living at home with mama; in his old room; on a twin bed. I mentioned before that sometimes in the black community adult children and parents continue to live with each other out of necessity or until the child is done with school, etc. But I firmly believe at a certain point every child, especially our sons, need to leave home. All male animals not only leave the nest, pride, or pack; they live as bachelors before they mate with a female. Every man should also leave home and experience bachelorhood as well. Men need to get their own apartments, run their own households, and have a little fun entertaining the ladies before they have families and settle down; 'cause no son of mine is turning my house into a motel, hotel, or Holiday Inn. My friend's man however, not only remained at home, he had some weird co-dependent relationship with his mother that totally interfered with his relationship with my friend.

This man did everything for his mother. He dropped her off and picked her up from work; he cooked for her; he took her shopping and to run all her errands. At first it seemed really sweet to see a man care so much for his mother. But as their relationship progressed, it became more and more difficult for my friend to deal with. I can't tell you how many Saturday nights my friend called me to say this dude just left her alone, candles burning, R.Kelly playing in the background, just because his mother called to say she needed a ride to church in the morning. I used to be like wow! Really? I know he loves his mother and it's great that he brings her to church every Sunday morning, but damn. Didn't he think if he wanted to have a romantic night with his lady that he would have said to his mother, "Hey Ma, I'm not going to be home until tomorrow, ask Brother or Sister Such 'n Such to pick you up for church in the morning".

Hello? You're a grown ass man.

Another friend of mine dated a man that would come over, watch her prepare and cook a five course meal and the minute she asked him to set the table for them to eat he would say, "My mom cooked spaghetti tonight, so I'll try to come back later." My friend used to be like, "Are you for real? You've been eating at your mom's table for three decades and you're leaving me for Monday night spaghetti?" Needless to say that relationship ended with my friend telling him to "get off his mother's tit already!" It was pretty funny. What else can you do but laugh at these things.

But the worst example of a "mama's boy" I can think of is my own experience with one. Keep in mind, all though I have separated these flaws in the brothers under different categories, a man can have any combination of these problems. He can be a player and a mama's boy, a homosexual and a jailbird, or a deadbeat dad and a dog (which ironically go hand in hand). Case in point, my "mama's boy" was my high school sweetheart and my eldest son's biological father.

I was fourteen when we met. At the time, I had no idea what a good boyfriend looked like. I didn't think there was anything wrong with his rude and disrespectful attitude toward his mother. I didn't think there was anything wrong with him cutting class, getting arrested for truancy, and other juvenile offenses. To tell you the truth, I wasn't thinking at all. But now that I am a mother, I know one thing for sure about raising my own sons. I know there's no way in hell if my son is rude and disrespectful to me am I going to keep him wearing the latest Jordan's and Polo shirts to school. There's no way when he sleeps out for days or gets thrown into juvey is he going to come home to find his bed neatly made and waiting for him. And I know for damn sure when he starts making babies at sixteen and continues to make them without ever getting a job, am I going to turn around and support all those damn kids. And that's exactly what his mother does.

The last time I spoke to him I said, "You have never supported my son. Haven't given me one dime to help raise him in fifteen years. God only knows how many over-night bags I packed and you never showed to pick him up. I asked you to call him at least once a week to say, "Hey son, how's life; how's school? But still you do nothing! Well, you're going to start doing something for my son as of now. If you don't start sending me some child support, I don't care if its ten dollars a week, I'm going to take you to court!"

Uugh! I was disgusted with him that day.

The thing that really pisses me off is anyone that knows me knows if I can avoid dialing 911 or avoid ever stepping foot into a government building, I would. I've told many of my friends to give their deadbeat baby father's a second chance before hauling him off to court because to me, being a father is not just about the money. If a man is low on cash, spending time with his children or just being there to help with homework, read them a story, or even throw a football around is just as important as the money they can provide. But I was frustrated to see my own philosophy not working for me just because this man was too selfish and too childish to even pick up a phone.

And you know what his response was to me now expecting him to start paying child support after fifteen years of nothing?

He said, "Listen honey, if you want child support you better speak to my mother because she's the one that pays all my child support".

U-n-b-e-l-i-e-v-a-b-l-e.

I was truly amazed that this thirty-something year old man had the ego and audacity to tell the mother of his child to go to *his mother* to take care of his responsibilities. He's not only a mama's boy, but a deadbeat dad that dogs women out and thinks he's some kind of player for getting away with it. And guess where he lives? In the same room he had when we were teenagers in high school. Really unbelievable.

After that conversation with my son's father, I told myself I'm done. I'm done talking to him. I'm done trying to foster a relationship between him and my son. I'm done. I don't have time to waste trying to raise a grown ass man when I have children of my own to worry about. I really don't need his money anyway. It was the principle.

It's clear to me now not only is my son's father a "mama's boy" of the worst kind, he also lives by the Deadbeat Dad Anthem: "It was your mother; your mother did this, your mother did that...that's why I couldn't be a father". And that's cool with me. I'll take all the blame now because in my heart I know I've done everything I could do to help this brother be a father. And I know I'm fulfilling my duty as a parent every day. I provide for my son, help him with his homework, cook his meals, wash his clothes, and try to live up to the countless other responsibilities of a parent. Whenever my son has a game and looks over at the stands, he sees my face; hears me cheering for him every time he scores or even gets his hands on the ball. Whenever he has a recital or graduation, mom is right there in the front row, clapping and hollering, "There goes my baby!"

I do hope and pray for my son's sake they develop a relationship one day. I'm married to a man that loves my son and treats him like his own. But deep down inside I know there's nothing like having a relationship with your own mother or father; somebody that looks like you, talks like you, walks like you. Even adopted children that have had great lives and families often look for their birth parents when they grow up. It's only natural to want to know who our parents are-good or bad.

The irony about the whole "mama's boy" situation is while these sons are playing "man of the house" for their mothers, any day mama finds a man of her own, she'll tell her son it's time to grow up and let mama have a life. The same woman that couldn't cut the apron strings so he could be a man for you, now has no problem living her life and urging her son to "get a life" of his own.

So our question remains, how do you love a black man when he's a mama's boy? The first thing you have to do is help this man cut the umbilical cord still tied to his mother. You're not trying to get in between them. You're his woman, she's his mother. Your job is to secure your position as the other important woman in his life. If a grown ass man's mother is still telling him who, what, when, where, and how to live his life, then she's not allowing her son to be a man. If you love him, really love him, it's up to you to help him become the great man he can be. Encourage him to make some decisions on his own while still showing love and respect for his mom and for your relationship as well.

A good son will always be there for his mother. If his mother is ever in crisis, of course he should be by her side and you should be right there with him. If the emergency room calls asking for her next of kin, grab the car keys and say, "C'mon babe, we need to go to the hospital now." Or if she calls and says a pipe in her basement burst and there's two feet of water gushing into the house, tell him you'll call a plumber while he goes over there and helps her get things cleaned up and situated. Be your man's backbone. Be his support.

But if a man's mother calls at ten o'clock at night and says, "I need you to come over and help me make these cookies I promised to bring to the church bake sale tomorrow", and he gets out of your warm bed to leave you and the kids home alone, you need to say to him, "Babe, it's late, don't go. Call your mother and tell her you'll buy her a few dozen cookies from whatever bakery and drop them off in the morning". He's still helping her. He's still being a good son. Even if she calls and says, "The downstairs toilet won't flush and I need you to come fix it now". He should be telling her to use the toilet upstairs and he'll be by to see if he can fix the broken one tomorrow.

Your man has to wean off his mother's breast at some point and the time is now. He's a man for God's sake! He has the ability to turn any woman into a mother with his own seed. His mother may never admit it, might never thank you for it, but when she sees her son being more independent and in control of his life, she'll know her work is done and he has a good woman on his side.

A LOOK IN THE MIRROR

It's hard to understand why a brother, who may or may not even live with his mother, still acts like a mama's boy and does everything she asks of him. The answer is simple. Communication. Mothers have no problem communicating with their children no matter how old that child is. A mother will let her son know her needs and expectations of him whether he wants to hear it or not. She's been doing it since he was a child. Didn't you know your mother expected your room to be clean and your chores to be done? When you didn't follow her instructions, didn't she let you know exactly how she felt about it and made sure you did what she asked?

Sometimes we sistahs don't communicate what we really need from our men. I'm not talking about buy me this or buy me that. I'm talking about what we need from him to feel loved and protected by him. What makes us feel secure in our relationship? What separates us from every other woman in his life, including his mother?

I don't know if it's a fear of ruining the relationship or maybe a fear that he may take what we're saying about his mother the wrong way. But if we don't tell a man how we feel about the situation, how will he know? Men are not mind readers. Half the time they tune out what we say.

And I'm not telling you to start acting like his mama now. You don't want to do that. You never want to do that.

Men hate that. All that "where you going; what you doing" every time your man gets up to take a piss will surely ruin your relationship. And you should never talk badly about or be disrespectful towards his mother either (remember that's where he came from). Just be a woman about your shit. You're an important part of his life too and you need to start acting like it. Use a little finesse on your man, make sure he knows what you need from him, and get him to follow through.

Remember ladies, a man's mama may have changed his dirty diapers and can still cook his favorite meal, but mama can't do *everything* he likes. So be his woman and let her be his mama.

Chapter 2

How to Love a Black Man when...He's a Player

"I'm not a player, I just crush a lot"-Big Punisher

Whether we're talking basketball, football, chess, checkers, or Monopoly... a player is someone playing a game. You have an opponent with the objective to score and win.

Millions of us sistahs think all men are "playing a game", that all men are "players", or feel like we have been "played" or "played out" by the brothers at one time or another. The brothers that admit to being players say "Don't hate the player, hate the game". What I couldn't figure out all these years is what game is it these brothers are playing?

I knew it's wasn't the dating game... 'cause these brothers are not trying to date us. It definitely ain't the newlywed game, 'cause these brothers are not trying to marry us. So I did some research (I discussed it with my husband and my brother) and I finally understand what game these brothers are playing and would like to share it with all my sistahs out there. It's called the GET PUSSY GAME. Experienced players use the advanced version, the CONQUER PUSSY GAME. But both versions have similar moves and rules with the same objective in mind: to attract as many women as possible, have sex with them, and continuously come up the new strategies to ensure they have commitment free sex with as many women as possible. And guess what ladies, whether you admit to it or not, you're playing the game too.

So what makes a man a player? Well, a player is a man on the hunt. He has all the tools and ammunition he needs to catch his prey, the pussy. You are his opponent because you have what he wants, the pussy. So whether it's his loot, bulging muscles, 26 inch rims, or new gear; a player has all the panty dropping ammunition he needs in order to attract you and initiate the first move.

You're on the hunt as well. You might tell yourself you're just going out to have fun with the girls; get away from the kids; or just cut loose after a stressful work week. But when you're wearing that tight, little freak 'em dress; with your 4 inch stilettos, boobies pushed up and out, "hair done, nails done, everything did"…it's game on. You didn't get all dressed up like that for your homegirls. Looking like that, you're attracting the very same men you say keep playing you, when in actuality you're the one playing yourself.

Don't get me wrong ladies. Of course some of us like to get dolled up and have a good time with the girls. But when you meet a man, especially in a club, and you guys smash on the first night, you can't possibly expect happily ever after to come from that. Now I didn't say you couldn't meet a man in the club. Clubs, like churches, gyms, parks, and even the supermarket are all places where two people could possibly meet and be attracted to each other. But meeting a man in the club is like giving him home court advantage. It's dark, the music is loud, and there is enough alcohol to cloud even the most intelligent woman's judgment. Once you give up the pussy, games over. He won. You might have been looking for Mr. Right, but ended up with Mr. Right now.

So don't play victim. Like I mentioned before, women play the game too. Lots of women in the club or bar have the same objective in mine as the men: to "get it in". Any woman can play the "Virgin Mary" role when she wants to. But we all have a little whore in us as well. And men know that. Ever seen a little show on MTV called the Jersey Shore? The guys go out every night looking for what they call "D-T-Fs", girls that are "Down-To-fuck". Likewise the girls are out looking for guys to "hook up with". Men sow their wild oats and so do today's women.

The problem is women are not built like men. They will always be better at this game than we are. We think because we have our degrees and can hold down the same jobs as men, we can be men, act like men. But if you didn't know one very important thing about men, especially the brothers it's this…a man can have sex with a woman, wash his dick off, and proceed with his day like nothing happened. Women are not like that. We're not men. We are emotional creatures. Sex is a physical and mental attachment for us.

Think about it this way. A man's sex organ hangs outside of his body, like a third leg. Better yet, think of a man's penis like a knife. A knife can be used to cut fruits, vegetables, beef, and bone. But guess what, no matter how many times you use a knife, you can just wash it off and use it again. You can't even tell what it was last used for. We can play detective and accuse a man of cheating because he stayed out late one night or didn't answer our phone calls and texts all day. Make ourselves totally crazy looking for clues and evidence. But unless we catch a man in bed with a woman, he can deny, deny, and deny our accusations until the day he dies. Even when we catch him with another woman, he might still be on some, "it wasn't me" mess. It can take a paternity test or positive STD result before some brothers will even consider admitting that they had sex with someone else. And some of them still try to deny the situation even then!

Our sex organs on the other hand are internal, tucked deep inside our bodies. We take a man inside us. We can't just wash him off. When a woman sleeps with multiple men she puts herself at risk for certain cancers or even worse, getting pregnant and not knowing who the father of her child is. We can actually get certain vaginal infections that are not necessarily sexually transmitted diseases, but can come from having too many different chemistries; too many different dicks in our vaginas, i.e. bacterial vaginitis or yeast infections. Ask your doctor if you don't believe me. Every man we're with leaves his imprint on our vaginas. And to all the sistahs that think you can have sex with other men and your man won't know… he knows. He might not be like, "I know you had sex last Tuesday at around 3pm with somebody else", but he can tell if things feel different since the last he was up in there, especially if he knows your body. So stop trying so hard to be a man and be the woman God created you to be.

◊

All men go through their player phase. At around eighteen to twenty-five years of age men are at their sexual peaks and have the stamina and appetites of lions in their prime. That's probably not a good time to be in a relationship with a man, especially if he is not ready to settle down. But black people always seem to want to settle down early. I hear black teenage boys calling their girlfriends "wifey". We have babies young and end up as baby mamas and daddies that hate each other. Men and women alike should be dating at that age (I didn't say fucking, I said dating), with the option to see other people. You're young. You're just getting to understand yourself and life in general. I think as long as people are honest with each other and communicate, no one will get hurt. You'll end up with some good friends and hopefully find your true love after that.

Unfortunately many of us sistahs fall in love with men that are in their "player phase" or men still "playing the field". Once we commit to or marry a man that is a player, what are the rules of the game then? This situation presents several problems. For one, the length of this phase differs for all men, especially the brothers. You have the young players out there just learning the game and the old pimps that can still get any woman they want. The other problem is that black men do not like to share their pussy. They're not going to tell you that they still sleep with other women because they don't want you to sleep with other men. It's too much for them to handle.

Well, I'm going to say somethings you might not like to hear, but it's for your own good.

I've heard a lot of sistahs say, "he cheated on me; that's the big no-no!" They break up with their man and a few years later it's "he cheated on me; that's the big no-no" and another relationship bites the dust.

It's funny how love is supposed to be this unconditional and selfless thing you give to someone. Yet the minute a man does something we don't like or if he doesn't give us want we want when we want it, we don't love him anymore. I guess there are some conditions to this love thing after all. Or are we simply mistaking love for lust? Mistaking being in love for infatuation? This may explain why a lot of us sistahs end up bitter and alone. Why we are unable to cope with the "big no-no" and end up living an "alternative" lifestyle.

Well, what I'm here to tell you ladies is this…all men are capable of the big "no-no". All men cheat.

If a man loves you, he loves you. He'll walk down the aisle. He'll put up with your nagging. He'll do whatever it takes to make you happy because you're his woman and he loves you. But if a man comes across a little booty he just can't refuse and he knows he's not going to get caught, he's going to go for it every time. Does that mean he doesn't love you? Of course not! Does that mean this other chick is better than you? No way! Most of the time it has nothing to do with us at all. It's just a man thing. A man can have sex with a woman and it won't mean anything to him beyond the physical act at that moment. We wouldn't even have to call it "cheating", which implies deception and fraud, if we would just accept men for what they are.

And what are men? Really they are such simple creatures at heart. They find so many different things about women sexy you can never really figure out what drives them to do the things they do. It could be another woman's obvious big booty or breasts. It could be her smile. It could be her laugh. It could be the eye contact and attention she gave him in the split second it took him to decide he was going to hit it, especially if those eyes are saying come get it. 'Cause let's face it, there are plenty of women out there that don't give a damn about his wife or girlfriend; they're D-T-F (Down-To-Fuck). And with so many brothers in jail and the other half of them gay, where else are these women going find a brother to lay the pipe. What are their alternatives? Dating outside their race? Becoming lesbians? This actually brings me to an important point about another "big no-no" amongst the sistahs- polygamy.

A lot of people think polygamy is just a selfish man having as many women as he wants when in actuality polygamy benefits the women as well. In traditional Afrikan culture, a man can take as many wives as he can afford. He has to provide all his wives with good homes and equal time. These women don't have to concern themselves with the shortage of black men in the world. They don't have to keep dating Mr. Wrong. And they don't have to opt for an abortion when Mr. Wrong gets them pregnant. They're married women. They have their own families and the added bonus of free babysitting next door.

Now I'm not saying we should all become polygamists. First of all this is not Africa. Our Afrikan minds have already been damaged and westernized by the white culture. We have too much ego and pride to ever openly share a man with another woman even though most of us are sharing him anyway. What will our friends and family think etc.? No, what I'm saying to you is this: if my man has sex with some other woman, I don't think that's a valid reason to break up my family. I don't think it's a valid reason to break up any family. I just don't see it.

My husband knows I'm a volatile and passionate person. I don't want to share him. I already share him with God and the two businesses he runs 50 miles away from our home. He knows I'd probably do something really crazy if I found out he was "cheating" on me. But cheating for me might be different from your definition of "cheating". Cheating for me is the intimacy, not the sex. If he goes out and falls in love with some other woman, comes home and tells me they're having a baby, it's over. We're married. I carry your babies now. What the fuck do you mean you love somebody else? You didn't tell this woman you were married or at least not looking for anything serious? But if my husband comes across a little booty he can't refuse, he knows he's not going to get caught, and he puts on a condom to protect my health and sanity, what the hell do I care. He's a man. He'll do it regardless. Why make him feel like he'll lose everything that really matters to him just because he's doing what's in his nature? Why stress myself out?

Some of you might say I'm living in ignorant bliss. But if I know these things about men and accept them, why am I being ignorant? I've cried enough tears about the "big no-no" to fill an Olympic sized swimming pool and it makes no sense to me to go through life like that anymore. If a man loves me, provides for our family, and lets everyone know he has his queen, what more can I ask?

It's hard enough for a man to commit to one woman, but he will if he loves you. That's one of the main reasons I think we should never propose marriage to a man. Yes we should let him know what we expect out of the relationship, our goals for the future. But if you don't let him decide, "Yes, I'm ready to marry this woman", he'll always be feeling like a caged animal with you holding the key to his freedom.

So how do you love a black man when he's a player? Simple. As I mentioned before all men go through their "player phase". Every man comes to a point in his life when he's ready to settle down. They start to look more than they touch and are content reminiscing about their "player days" instead of still playing. They can't deal with the headaches of juggling multiple women; they know they're the oldest one at the club, etc. So if you love this man, see his indiscretions for what they are, and believe he's worth it, wait it out. It's kind of like riding out the teenage years with your kids. When our children become teenagers they put us through hell for at least 4-6 years and then one day transform back into the sweet angels that loved us just for baking them cookies. Men are the same way. When the player phase is over you'll end up with the man you love and a man that loves you back. So ride it out my sistahs. Ride or die.

Another thing I want us to keep in mind is some men continue to play the field because they don't want to get hurt or "played" either. Let us not forget about all the gold-diggers, heart breakers, and man-eaters out there that play the game too. Some of our brothers come from the same broken homes and have the same broken hearts that we do. They have their fears and insecurities about relationships too. I think we forget a woman can be a man's greatest weakness; his love for women his greatest flaw. A man will make a fool of himself for a woman. Men fight for women. Men die for women. Didn't Adam eat the apple because Eve convinced him to do it despite his better judgment? Didn't Prince Edward VIII of England give up the crown for an American woman he was in love with? If you have ever seen the movie Scarface and think Tony Montana killed Frank just for drug money, think again.

So be patient with the brothers and show them some love. Whether they admit it or not, they want our love…they need our love…they deserve it.

A LOOK IN THE MIRROR

And while you're waiting for this man to basically grow up. Remember this. Keep your game tight. A lot of us sistahs think being married or in a committed relationship gives us a license to let ourselves go. Trust me on this one, the "player phase" will last a lot longer if the attractive woman he met, that worked out at least twice a week, cooked and cleaned for him, and wore sexy lingerie now has a muffin top, wears sweats to bed, and complains about doing household chores. Even if you're full figured and fabulous, it's unacceptable to go from 200lbs to 300lbs just because you have a man now. It's unacceptable to stop doing your hair and nails if that's what you were doing when you guys met. You don't expect a man to get bored with you and want to play the field when you're acting like that? Any man with common sense knows a woman's weight changes with time and pushing out babies. Sometimes we get behind in the housework, we've been working overtime, or the kids are driving us nuts. Typical of the "mommy phase". But if you're not close to being the same woman he fell in love with, don't be surprised when he still goes out on the hunt. Men love the hunt. It's a sport. It's a game. It excites the player in them. It's our job to make sure we're the prey our men keep coming after. So keep your game tight sistah. Keep it tight.

Chapter 3

How to Love a Black Man when…He's a Dog

"Why must I be like that, why must I chase the cat…ain't nothing but the dog in me…"-George Clinton

Dogs are the most loyal creatures on the planet. Man's best friend. When you walk through your front door, there they are waiting to greet you; doing back flips and cartwheels just to make you smile. They play when you want them to play. They sit when you want them to sit. Even on your worst days they stay right by your side, giving you all the doggy love and emotional support they can muster. Their love is unconditional and all they want to do is please their master. Sounds like an ideal relationship.

Some dogs can even find missing children, sniff out bombs, and detect cancer! They're four legged heroes! So why do black women often refer to men our men as dogs in a derogatory way. Let's consider a dog's behavior when they're not licking our faces or cuddled up at our feet.

We know that dogs are cute, cuddly, and loyal. They have their own little personalities and qualities that make them members of the family. What we often forget about our dogs is that they are animals. And like all animals, their behaviors are based on doing what is natural to them. Case in point, when a dog sees another dog in the street, they are basically star struck. They're like "bow wow, who is that fine canine?!" They start barking and howling; excitedly pulling you as close as possible just to get next to that dog. You're thinking "oh how cute, they want to make friends". But if you know anything about dogs, you know dogs want a lot more than to "make friends" when they approach each other. For one thing, just by sniffing another dog's behind, a dog can tell if is it a male or female dog, is the dog healthy, and what kind of attitude or temperament the dog has. They can even recognize if they already know the dog. Male dogs are usually more macho towards each other. It's either, "hey man what's up" and they're cool or it's "what the fuck are you looking at" and it's a fight. It's all about checking the other dog out.

So what do we suppose is happening when it's a female-male dog encounter? Of course that male dog is checking that female dog out. Is she cute? How are those hind quarters looking? What's her height and weight? And she's checking him out too… what breed is he? How long does that tail of his hang? They're both checking out the merchandise to see if they like each other. If the female likes the male, better believe she'll turn round and round to make sure he gets a good look at her merchandise and a good whiff of that ass too. If she doesn't like him she may just growl, letting him know to back up, I'm with my master right now, go bark up some other tree. Whatever she does, that male dog will put up with it, cause all he really wants to know is, "is this bitch in heat and how can I get some". Sound familiar?

Lots of us sistahs meet men everyday under similar circumstances. You could be just walking down the street minding your own business. Or maybe you're at the bar getting your drink on; in the club getting your dance on; you could even be in church getting your pray on and here comes a brother sniffing around. He's like the cute puppy in the pet-shop window just begging you to take him home.

So what are we really saying when we call our men dogs? In the previous chapter we discussed men that are players and the men in relationships that still "play the field". Some of you probably think a man that's a player is the same as a man that dogs you out. But I totally disagree. For one thing, a player doesn't think he's doing anything wrong. His actions and words tell you, "baby this is how it is…this is who I am…leave or live with it". It's how you receive his message that makes the difference in your relationship. A real player can walk around with a woman on each arm and one waiting in the back seat of his ride if he wants to; the Hugh Hefners and P.Diddys of the world. Of course not all the players out there have Playboy/Badboy money and we wonder why these women are really with these men. But like I said before, we play the game too.

No, a man that's a dog is a different kind of man. A man that's a dog will have sex with your sister or cousin just because he can. A man that's a dog lies, lies, lies about everything even when the truth is standing at the front door with his secret love child. He says things like, "That wasn't my car you saw in Kim's driveway; or it wasn't me coming out of that motel room."

We usually refer to our man as a dog after we find out he has "cheated" on us multiple times with multiple women. Or when we find out he has multiple baby mamas and half his children are "project twins". He's definitely a dog after he has given us a few STDs. And the biggest sign our man is a dog, despite all his dirty ways, unbelievably, this man continues to profess his love and devotion for us. Just like a dog.

And why do our men behave this way? Simple. Because like dogs, doggish men actually want to please us. They really do love us and don't want to lose our love and affection for them. They're like the pit-bulls that snap and bite they're owners. They don't even understand why they do the things they do; why they're so reckless with it. When they have their indiscretions they feel guilty and try to cover them up like a dog that just ate the meatloaf you left out on the counter. The guilt is written all over their faces.

So are men really just four legged beasts pissing all over our hearts, chewing away at our souls, all the while fucking every bitch they see in the street? Or are our men, like our dogs, doing what is natural to them?

To understand our man's behavior, we must first examine our own. When you started seeing this man, he said he didn't have a girlfriend or a wife hiding somewhere. He told you he had "friends" and hoped you two could be "friends" and "get to know each other". That's a pretty honest statement for a man to make. Or it could be a big, fat lie and he has women stashed in every borough. Either way, this man is trying to warn you that he sleeps with other women and isn't looking for a commitment right now. It's the big sign on the gate that says BEWARE OF DOG. But like most women and other people that get bit by dogs, we ignored it.

Sure enough, after a couple of dinners, a few movie dates, maybe a long, romantic walk on the beach, and hours of kissy face over the phone, now he's *your man*. Not to mention you let him do it to you doggy-style, so now he's really *your man*.

And then it happens. You pop up at his house unexpectedly because you're *his woman* and find him there with another woman. Better yet, ya'll are hanging out and you decide to answer his cell while he's in the bathroom because he's *your man* and your greeted by the sultry voice of some other chick on the line or accidently see her budonk-a-donk in the picture she just texted him. All hell breaks loose and suddenly a brother that was just following his nature is nothing but a dirty dog. It's a drama filled roller coaster ride for the two of you from that point on. You no longer trust a man that was straight with you when you guys started kicking it. And now that you're all caught up and feeling him, you're giving him ultimatums as to how he has to live his life in order to keep you.

Let's be honest with ourselves ladies. At what point in time did this man say he was ready to be *your man*? Of course you guys are getting closer and having a good time. He would've stop calling after you let him hit it if he wasn't having a good time and you wouldn't be blabbing to all your homegirls how much you like him if you weren't haven't having a good time too. But other than fun and good times, what changed since the day you two met and he told you he was looking for a "friend"? Did he ever say he was going to stop seeing other people? Did you guys ever discuss taking your relationship to the next level?

I recently read Steve Harvey's Act Like a Lady, Think Like a Man..., which you should all read after you finish reading my book if you haven't already done so, LOL. And even though Steve has been married and divorced several times, he said a lot of real shit in there. The most important message I took away from the book is that a lot of times we women do not set any standards for ourselves or have any requirements of a man before we are willing to give him our everything. And by everything I mean our time, our affections, our bodies, years of good cooking from our mama's kitchens...everything. And why do we do this? Because in our minds things are going great; we're playing the role of the best girlfriend and best potential wife he could ever have. So why wouldn't he commit to me? But you never did ask him if he stopped seeing other people even though you have. You didn't tell him you wanted to be his girl, instead of just a booty call. We sistahs always assume men think and feel the same way we do. And you know what they say about those of us who assume shit.

So how do you love a black man when he's a dog? The first thing we must realize is if you're with a man and his actions show you he's not ready for a commitment, he's not. Forget what he says while you two are all cuddled up. It's his actions. A man with doggish tendencies will lie and pretend to want a commitment just to please you. He does everything he can to hide his dirt. He doesn't mean to hurt you. He's just too selfish to let you go.

This can be a really painful situation. This is when love hurts. Back home we have a saying, "once bitten, twice shy"; meaning, if you get bit by a dog once, it was an accident. If you let that dog bite you again, you're a fool. Sometimes you just have to face the fact that he's a dog girlfriend. Leave his ass.

But if you're already in love with this man, want to wake up to his cute little face and can't imagine not having him to cuddle up with at night, remember one thing...all dogs want to please their master. So be his master. Get that dog trained.

Dogs have a pack mentality. It's where their loyalties lie. They're always looking to the leader of the pack, the dog that is the strongest, to provide the most stability and comfort to their lives. In the case of dogs and humans, the human must be the "leader of the pack" or "master". A man that's a so-called "dog" will eventually pick the woman that stands out the most from his "pack of women". She's the calm, patient, dominant "master" that knows him the best; knows how much he needs her in his life. Sistahs that know this, and recognize the good qualities these brothers do have despite their doggish ways, don't give up on them. So don't you give up on these brothers either.

Keep in mind for hundreds of years in this country black men were used as breeding machines encouraged to have sex with as many black women as possible with no commitment to the women or children left in their path, just like a roaming dog. That's damage at the cellular level. Sorry to say it's still in their DNA; it's the dog in them. It takes a strong woman to deal with this defective behavior. So remember sistahs, our men, when acting like dogs need you to lead them to be the good men we all know they can be. Only you can show him how good life can be when he has a nice home, a bowl full of food, and someone to scratch all his itches!

A LOOK IN THE MIRROR

It's so easy for us sistahs to call a black man a dog when he exhibits certain behavior. What's interesting about that is it has become even easier for a brother to call a black woman a female dog whenever he feels like it. A bitch.

When I was growing up you better not dare call anyone's mother or sister a bitch. You better not even open your mouth to say anything against a black child's mother, especially a son. Those were automatic fighting words. Yet every rapper today refers to many mothers and sisters as all kind of bitches and hoes. And our children are listening to them and doing the same thing. What is happening to the black community?

Let us first address the characteristics of a bitch or female dog. Bitches are more independent than male dogs. They tend to want to be the alpha dog, the one in control, the leader of the pack. Bitches can be very stubborn and fiercer than a male dog despite their breed or size. They are less affectionate than male dogs often seeking affection from you, but walk away when they have had enough. And of course they are extremely territorial. Sound familiar?

So what is a man really telling you when he calls you a bitch? A man will usually refer to a woman as a bitch not just because of her behavior, but more so if he feels disrespected by that woman. And sorry to say sistahs, a lot of us are very disrespectful towards black men. We want a man, but we don't know how to treat a man. So many of us think we are in control of or head of the household just because we have a bigger paycheck. It's our way or the highway. We complain when they don't spend time at home, but don't bother to make sure home is a clean, comfortable, loving environment where a man can rest his head and heart after taking a beating in this white man's world. We have no problem getting in their faces; embarrassing them in front of their friends or at their work; or telling them "nigga you ain't shit" when we see them struggling. We demand that they put all their eggs in our basket and then have no problem throwing those eggs all over their face.

And please don't think I'm on my high horse preaching to the choir. I might be writing a book now, but it didn't start out that way. I've spend thousands of hours on the phone, writing in my journal, or just hanging out with my girlfriends trying to figure black men out; why they do the things they do; and how to love them despite it all? But lately I've been trying to figure out why none of my friends and so many other sistahs I know are not in stable relationships; why I haven't been to a single wedding in over twelve years; and why even though I'm married to a man that loves me, I continuously sabotage our relationship over trivial matters. I had to take a look in the mirror. And I'm just asking ya'll to do the same thing.

Black families and relationships are in turmoil because sorry to say, we're acting like white folks. So caught up in the fairytale of love meaning romance and sex, we have forgotten what black love is all about. Black love is spiritual. Black love is a oneness. Black love is showing kindness and compassion towards each other even when we're angry or disagree. Black love is about respect. Black love nourishes our souls and helps us fulfill our destinies in life. Have you forgotten we survived slavery together? Segregation? The crack epidemic? We do it together.

Black love is a beautiful thing.

Of course there are some very disrespectful brothers out there that will call a black woman a bitch without provocation. They obviously have no home training or have some serious issues with women that may need professional intervention. I just want us sistahs to take responsibility for our own behaviors and actions.

If you have a tendency towards the characteristics that describe a "bitch" or female dog as discussed on the previous page, take some time to change that energy in your life. Black women don't need to be bitches. We need to be the Queens we were designed to be. Take it from a sistah that knows. If you keep disrespecting your man and you're out here acting like a bitch...don't be surprised when you wake up one day alone in a bed full of fleas.

Chapter 4

How to Love a Black Man when He is a Scrub or Deadbeat

Dad

"No…I don't want no scrub, a scrub is a guy that can't get no love from me…hanging out the passenger side of his best friend's ride trying to holler at me…"-TLC

One of the most strategic maneuvers white folks used on us to ensure not only the longevity of slavery, but the lasting mental, psychological, and emotional scars of such an institution, was to separate and destroy the black family.

Even before they threw us in the bottom of those ships they decided to separate husbands from wives, fathers from sons, mothers from daughters, and sisters from brothers. Add to that the confusion of being sold by your own people or stolen in the middle of the night; chained up and thrown into the bottom of a dark, overcrowded ship; the white man also decided to mix different tribes together so we couldn't effectively communicate with each other. If we survived being transported across the world as cargo we were weighed, processed, categorized, and sold to the highest bidder. When you finally got to the plantation you started your new existence. No longer a man. No longer a woman. No longer someone's son or daughter; a king or queen; a pillar in your community. You were a slave. A slave.

In the early 1800s when Great Britain finally decided to end the slave trade and ban the importation of African slaves to the west, white folks in America came up with their own idea on how to continue what they saw as a thriving economic force in their New World. If they couldn't import slaves, they would manufacture their own. I recently read an article in Time magazine that stated, "Slaves were the single largest financial asset in the United States of America, worth over $3.5 billion in 1860 dollars…" Billions!

So naturally, being the good business men that they were, many plantation owners set up breeding farms where they selected slaves based on their complexions, size, strength, and other physical attributes they considered desirable to make the new "super" slaves. This would explain why we dominate every professional sport and the entertainment industry today.

These new offspring, like all slaves, were "Massa's" property. A black man wasn't a man, so that wasn't his son or daughter running around the plantation; that was "Massa's" property. You weren't a mother. You were a breeding wench and that was one of your pups, not your child. You could wake up one morning and find your child gone. "Massa" fed you, "Massa" clothed you, and you carried "Massa's" last name.

A lot of people say "forget slavery, slavery is over". Funny no one ever tells a Jewish person to forget the Holocaust or a Native American to forget the millions that were slaughtered in European massacres. But we should forget slavery. How many black people do you know with the last name Jackson, Williams, or Johnson? How many black people do you know still letting "Massa" raise their children in foster homes; or supporting their children in the form of welfare and food-stamps? How many black men are warehoused in so-called "correctional facilities" similar to plantations? How can we forget something that still happens today?

◊

Did you know giraffes used to have short necks? Like most animals in Africa, giraffes are vegetarian. They have to compete with the zebras, gazelles, and hundreds of other animals for the best foliage. In the wild it's all about survival of the fittest. So when the giraffes saw all the beautiful, green leaves growing high in the trees, they started stretching their necks to reach the abundance of food hanging above their heads. Lo and behold, their offspring evolved with longer necks and now all giraffes are born that way. The same evolutionary process has occurred with the black man due to slavery. After hundreds of years of eliminating their roles as husbands and fathers; providers to their families; many black men carry the defective gene of being a scrub and/or deadbeat dad.

◊

Any real man wants to feel like a king; king of his castle, king of his domain. A man wants security. A man wants to respect himself and feel respected by others. Any man that is satisfied sitting around his mama's house all day with no money in his pocket and no plan on how to make some is not a man, he a scrub. Any man sweet talking all the ladies with plenty of time on his hands to take them out on the town without ever reaching into his pocket to pay a tab or bill because he's broke all the time is not a man, he's a scrub. Any frontin'ass; talking shit; full of excuses; ain't got his own place; ain't got his own ride brother out here thinking he's *the man* because he's been getting away with this behavior is not a man, he's a scrub.

So if you're man is always in between jobs; constantly borrowing your money or your car because he doesn't have his own; always promising to pay for the movie "next time"...RUN! He's a scrub: a modern day slave still happy letting "Massa" take care of things for him.

The sad thing about the situation is these men are comfortable being scrubs. They are happy in their unprogressive state. Just chillin' like a motherfucker; they have given up the fight. They tell the other slaves, "don't run, we got it good here". No man is free from life's responsibilities, yet they revel in the lack of responsibility in their own lives. These are not men. They're slaves!

You might be paying for everything because you love him; because you're hoping he'll change, hoping he'll step up. But really all you're doing is enabling his behavior and perpetuating his slave mentality.

The worst thing is to do is fall in love with a man like this. He promises you a ring he will never buy. Most likely, he thinks he's a player, sleeps with other women that help support him, and has a bunch of kids he doesn't take care of. Then you get pregnant. You're hoping the love he has professed for you will make him step up, but he still doesn't. Now you've not only depleted your savings account and wasted years of your life with this man, you're stuck with a deadbeat as the father of your child.

We have to do a better job at picking the men we choose to have children with. A lot of sistahs pick their men the same way animals do. Female animals always look for the best physical attributes in their potential mates. Female birds choose the males with the brightest feathers; a lioness chooses the lion that is the strongest and appears to be the healthiest to mate with. It's just like the sistahs who say, "If I have a baby with him, my baby will be cute" or "my baby will have good hair, etc." Of course we have to be attracted to each other, but we should be choosing potential husbands and fathers based on more substantial qualities like altruism, kindness, patience, respect, and responsibility. 'Cause you know what... a mother lioness can't go back to the lion complaining she doesn't have enough zebra meat to feed her cubs or that the watering hole is dry. Once a lion breeds a lioness, his job is done. He goes back to living his life and being king of the jungle. Of course he plays his role as leader and protector of the pride, but it's the lioness's responsibility to care for and support her cubs. So yes, the lion is handsome and majestic, but is he the kind of father you want for your child? Now a penguin on the other hand may not have the sexy of a lion, but they do mate with you for life and help with every aspect of child rearing including sitting on and protecting the eggs until they hatch! Maybe we need to give some of the penguins out there a chance.

I mentioned before the Deadbeat Dad Anthem: "It was your mother; your mother did this, your mother did that...that's why I couldn't be a father". Another sign a man is a scrub or deadbeat dad includes describing the mother of his children as "crazy, angry, bitter, etc." despite the fact that he is not helping her to raise his own children. Watch out! Scrubs that have children live by the Deadbeat Dad anthem. They feel no responsibility towards their children because "Massa" will help you to take care of things. It's fine with them if they are listed as "missing" or "absent" on their child's welfare application. They are glad to know WIC will pay for the milk, Medicaid will pay for the doctor bills, and Public Assistance will pay the rent. These are the men that unfortunately have to be taken to court to support their own children. Then they say, "Well, you get child support so I'm doing anything else". They let you do all the work of parenting the child then show up 18 years later wanting to be "friends" with their children.

Scrubs and/deadbeat dads are the same brothers that actually think if a judge orders some ridiculous amount of support, like $25 dollars a week, that that fulfills their role as a father. I wonder if these brothers have any idea how much it costs to care for and raise a child? I've never gotten my paycheck and said "Well, I'm only spending $25 this week on these damn kids of mine". Children need food, clothing, and shelter; that food has to be cooked; those clothes need detergent to get washed; a home needs to be maintained; they use electricity, heat and hot water; they need haircuts and hairdo's; they need braces; they need music lessons; they need uniforms for their sporting events; they need tuition for college. It costs something like $200,000 dollars to give your child a fighting chance in this world. Black children born into poverty remain poor and disadvantaged throughout their lives because "Massa" is still raising them; not their parents, not their fathers. Just like back on the plantation.

You have to wonder what would make a man behave this way. Abandoning his own child, a part of himself, his greatest responsibility in life? There are brothers sitting in jail right now for not paying child support either because they couldn't get a job, couldn't keep a job, or just don't have the skills or mentality to create one. This is not the natural behavior of an Afrikan man. This is who America has groomed the Afrikan man to be. This is a slave. This is what a nigger looks like.

The 13th Amendment may have ended slavery, but a lot of us still need to "emancipate ourselves from mental slavery"-Bob Marley

Don't get me wrong, there are wonderful single mothers out there doing their thing. These sistahs are providing for and raising their children the best way they know how. But we can't overlook the importance of a child having his/her father or at least a father figure in their lives.

Raising a boy is something any mother can do with patience and prayer. I have four sons, believe me I know! Raising a boy to be a man is a whole different ball game. A father shows his son how to be a man. A father can relate to his son on a man to man level. He can be a wonderful example, guiding his son, teaching him responsibility, teaching him how to find and treat a lady. Or at least he's there to say, "son don't make the same mistakes I did, I want better for you".

Mothers teach their daughters how to be women. But fathers teach their daughters how to be treated like a woman. A father gives his daughter the perfect example of unconditional love and shows her how she should be treated by a man. It makes a big difference in a young woman's relationships with men if when a potential suitor arrives for their date, Daddy's there to say, "You better take care of my little girl or else (meaning my girl, not yours, until you have proven yourself)".

Studies now prove the way a father treats his expectant wife or girlfriend has a profound effect on the development of a child. Children really do need both their mothers and fathers.

◊

So how do you love a black man when he's a scrub or deadbeat dad? I know I said to run from a brother like this. Sometimes that is the only solution. You can never do more for a person than they are willing to do for themselves. You're love for him and tolerance of this behavior is keeping him from becoming a man. This man has to find his manhood on his own. He needs time to grow up, get his life together and become a real man before he can have a relationship with any woman or be a father to his children. Even if the man you're dating is not the father of your kids, you should make it clear to any man you date that you can't be with him if he doesn't support and make time for his children. Hopefully he will be a better man for it, if not for you, for the next sistah that comes along.

But if you truly love a man that is a scrub/deadbeat and can't let him go, here is another solution. Build together. Have you ever wondered why whenever we need temporary assistance from the government in the form of housing, welfare, food-stamps, or Medicaid that the father of our child must be UNKNOWN or ABSENT in order for us to receive benefits? Why can't we have a responsible, employed man in our lives and still get the help we need from our government until we get back on our feet? The answer is clear to me. It's because this government knows that stronger families in the black community will strengthen our people as a whole. They don't want that. They never did. They separated us on the ships, they separated us on the plantations, and they're still doing it today. They want our men to be scrubs, deadbeat dads, and jailbirds so that our sons can be scrubs, deadbeat dad, and jailbirds. They want to make it seem as though they are trying to help the black community with their "programs and funding" when really they are the ones holding us back; keeping us dependent on the "Massa" so we never leave the plantation. They want to keep us dependent. They want us to be slaves. Who really makes the money from all these so-called "social welfare" programs? Who really benefits from keeping black families dependent on the government anyway?

A few months ago, George Bush was in the news promoting his book and he commented that "the most disgusting moment" of his presidency was when Kanye West said he didn't care about black people. Let me just drop a little science on you right now. If there is a tsunami, earthquake, hurricane, tornado, or any such disaster on the other side of the world, the first people that are there to help are THE AMERICANS. Yet when poor, black Americans were suffering right across state lines, there was no help from this government for them. The news actually referred to the people of New Orleans 9th Ward, citizens of this country, as "refugees". Do you think if Hurricane Katrina had hit Orange County or Beverly Hills the "refugees" would have waited weeks for assistance from their own government?

We can't keep letting "Massa" raise our families. We can't keep thinking this government will ever compensate us for the evils they have inflicted on our people; especially our men. If you're dating a scrub, you need to help him become a man; help him find his Afrikan spirit. You need to make this man a partner in your life, not your dependent. If he really loves you he's not going to want you to struggle. He's not going to use you. He will step up. Making him your partner will help his natural instincts to be provider and father kick in and break his slave/scrub mentality. Men always want to do better when a good woman is behind them. They want to make their families proud. If he needs to go to school, make a plan for you to work fulltime while he attends classes or a trade school. When he's working, you can go back to school. Help each other. Be a family. That's what black love is all about.

And since we talked about all the scrubs and deadbeats out there, I want to take time to mention all the brothers on the opposite end of the spectrum: the work-a-holics. If your man is a total work-a-holic he definitely needs all your love and support too. Men that work two and three jobs, travel for work, or work 60-70 hours a week need to know all the effort they put into building a future with you is not taken for granted. I know it gets lonely. It's frustrating. And sometimes the material things and financial security he's working for just doesn't keep you warm enough at night. Just keep in mind when a man has a plan and a destiny to fulfill, nothing is going to stop him. You complaining about him being away all the time only makes it harder for him to focus on the task at hand: securing a future for himself and your family. Don't think he doesn't want to be home with you and the kids, he does. Don't think he doesn't miss you too; he misses you more than he is able to express. Sometimes a man just has to do what he has to do. Real men make certain sacrifices in order to achieve their goals in life. Remember that the situation is temporary. Even if temporary means ten years of him hustling or grinding at whatever his craft may be. Your love and patience will pay off for both of you in the in the end. Just keep loving each other. Peace.

A LOOK IN THE MIRROR

"YOU ARE NOT THE FATHER!"

So I'm home on maternity leave and I discover that every morning, women across the country are facing a huge dilemma. They made a huge mistake or have a terrible secret…they don't know who fathered their children and have come on national television to figure it out. My first thought is we (women) have one period and one egg (maybe two if it's twins) every month. Yet these women are showing up with two, three, four, even five men on one episode I saw, trying to figure out which man fathered their child! My second thought is…you accidentally slept with at least five men in one month without protection? Two of them are cousins, the other two best friends. You kept it a secret the whole time you were pregnant. Or maybe you told one of the men he was the father and the other two or three they weren't. But now that the child is born you can't tell for sure? Not to mention you put yourself at risk of contracting and/or spreading sexually transmitted diseases all over the place? Are you for real?

If this show is any indication of how the majority of women behave, is it any wonder why men fear monogamy and commitment? Is it really that hard to understand why men are quick to say, "That's not my kid" and walk away when they know how trifling and scandalous women can be? The part that really kills me is when these women come out on the stage they are 100% sure a certain man is the father. They're in this man's face telling him he's the worse man in the world; a total deadbeat and scumbag for not supporting her children up until now. Then the test results are revealed proving this man is not the father and the woman runs off stage shocked and embarrassed; screaming and crying as if she had no idea sleeping with multiple men could lead to something like this.

On the flip side, if the guy is proven to be the father, they're still in his face, yelling and screaming, "I told you *you* were the father, I told you!" Then they start doing the latest dances cheered on by the audience as though they just won the lotto. This display is followed by more yelling and threats to take the man to court for child support. It's an unbelievable sight.

I do give these women some credit for having the courage to bring a child into the world under these circumstances. There was a controversial anti-abortion ad posted on a billboard in New York City a few weeks ago that said something like "the womb is a dangerous place for an African-American child to be". We sistahs are always under the microscope and either being portrayed as welfare mothers or according to Don Imus, "nappy headed hoes". It's hard to say whether or not when a woman doesn't know who fathered her child what choice she should make. I don't think it's anyone's business but that woman's what choice she makes regardless of her situation. I only mention this issue to point out that as black women, we have to be more careful with our bodies and make better choices about the men we share our bodies with. We want our men to respect us. We want our men to love and commit to us. We want our men to be our protectors and providers; husbands and fathers; to be real men. Yet we are not being real woman. Being sexy and sleeping around does not make a woman a real woman. The clothes you wear does not make a woman a real woman. How much money you can make does not make a woman a real woman. A real woman holds her virtue and sets high standards for herself. She carries herself like a queen. She commands respect and respects those around her. She is strong when she needs to be and has an independent spirit. A real woman can contribute to her household and keep it clean. She is daughter, sister, wife, and mother with every step she takes. A real woman is a sight to behold.

If you are facing the kind of baby mama/baby daddy drama I see on TV without the cameras being there, you have to make a change. You guys were once in love with each other. You had a child together. If things didn't work out for whatever reason and now you can't stand the sight of each other that has nothing to do with the child. Unfortunately this is what happens when we focus on sex and romance as the foundation of our relationships instead of spirituality and family structure. Our children become collateral damage in these situations and it's not right. For their sake, we must find some common ground with their fathers so the child benefits from having both parents in their lives. I struggle with this issue myself. But unless we change our men never will. None of us are perfect. Neither are our men. But let us strive towards that perfection together. Be a queen and you'll make your man a king. Find your MAAT: SELF, FAMILY, AND COMMUNITY. PEACE.

Chapter 5

How to Love a Black Man when…he's a Hustler

"America doesn't respect anything but money. What our people need is a few millionaires."-Madame C.J. Walker

It's so easy to fall for a hustler. Whether he's slanging crack-rock, dope, or boot-leg CDs, when a black man hustles for his loot, he is a man in control of his own destiny. This man is sure he has finally found a way to rule the world or at least taking the necessary steps to get there. He exudes that confidence, sells it to you, and when you fall in love with him, you're a loyal customer for life.

The Criminal Justice Department sees these men as a dangerous entity in our society; a problem. Black men are considered dangerous just for being black. So when you have black men making tax-free money and getting power and respect in their communities- it's a big problem. If they can take over their communities, they can take over the world. And that's a bigger problem.

There is nothing wrong with a black man wanting to make a lot of money and securing his place in this world. The problem is how he does it. Drug dealers make a lot of money in their communities, but they are destroying those communities at the same time. There's increased violence over the control of certain blocks, innocent people are caught in the cross-fires, and once productive black people are left walking around as crack-heads and dope fiends unable to care for themselves or their families. Violence and murder are accepted as casual occurrences in the hood, our precious lives dispensable. I don't know how many more crime scene tapes, candle light vigils, and RIP shrines it's gonna take before we stop the madness? I don't know how many more brothers and sistahs have to die before we stop the violence amongst our own? The only thing I know is that it needs to stop. It has to stop.

The fucked up thing about this whole shit is, there are no gun factories or gun shops open in black communities. There are no poppy fields or coca plantations growing in the hood. Exactly how do these dangerous items get into the hands of our brothers (and some sistahs too)? Why are our men going to prison for using the resources available to them?

The other fucked up thing about this situation is these men are some of the smartest people in the world. Under different circumstances they could have been mathematicians, scientists, or CEOs of Fortune 500 companies. But you see when a man is starving...not I missed breakfast this morning starving. I'm talking starving for his dignity and pride, starving for self- respect, starving for better jobs to provide for his family, better schools to educate his children, a better way of live; just to wake up and feel like a man... he'll do whatever it takes to make that dollar. "By any means necessary". Even if those means are hurting his friends and neighbors or destroying his community; a man will do whatever it takes to escape starvation. And those same friends and neighbors will cash out their food stamps, pawn all their stuff; borrow, beg, lie, cheat, and steal to help themselves escape from that feeling of starvation as well; never mind the depression, PTSD, and other mental disorders created by living in the impoverished and violent environment the hood easily provides. It's a fucked up situation.

A lot people don't know the slaves use to get high too. Why the hell do you think so many of them stop trying to escape? How was the cocaine getting on the plantations? Who were our dealers back then?

So yes, you can tell I too was in love with a hustler.

◊

I had never met a man like Charles. Smart, handsome, and ambitious; he was my everything. Whenever I walked into a room he was genuinely happy to see me. Never told me I was too dark or too skinny; didn't care if my hair was nappy or straight. He just loved me for me. You can't put a price on that.

Coming to America as a poor immigrant from JA was more than a dream for him. It was his one opportunity to change his life and make things better for his family. Whether it meant getting paid off-the-books at a construction site, driving a taxi, or selling a little weed on the corner, he was going to make it in this country. He was going to make it by any means necessary.

Charles was a good dude. But his ambitions and desire for more lead him away from making a few extra dollars on the corner to becoming one of New York's most notorious drug dealers. The first time he told me to "put this away" and dropped a warm gun in my hand I knew he was trouble, knew he was a dangerous man. But I was already in love. I was down for him and he was down for me. His jealous and controlling ways, frustrations about the business, and paranoia about his competitors became my own. Our love was the real deal.

Then there were the perks. I had every material thing I could possibly want. Too much when I think about it now. The cars and clothes; the expensive jewelry; plush carpeting in every room; marble floors in the kitchen; leather sofas in my living room; and a king-sized brass beds in my boudoir made me feel like a queen. I even had a ridiculous doll collection that was the envy of every little girl that came to our house. There was money to blow and we blew it.

And even though he worked long nights making deals and even longer days pushing the product he always had time for me. We had breakfast together every morning, romantic dinners at Sammy's on City Island, and went to Woodlawn to put fresh flowers on his mother's grave every Sunday. He always tried to do the right thing.

Life was good. But things in the Big Apple were getting rotten fast. It was 1989 and the height of the crack epidemic. People were getting robbed left and right, packages weren't coming through, and the fiends were more ruthless in their quest for the next hit. Almost every week you heard about someone getting shot or being dead. Reagan declared a war on drugs. But the war *for* drugs was even realer.

I knew it was time for a change but Charles wasn't ready to change.

I would say to him, "Why don't we just leave it all?"

But how could he just leave.

Or "Why don't you take some of this money and open something legit?"

But to him this was legit; "too legit to quit". Selling dope was how he made his money. It was his business, his craft. They didn't call him "Doc" for nothing. His plan was to make enough money this year so he could retire and be out. That was the plan. He always came through and he would come through with this too. He just needed one more year. Just one more year.

So I went along with the plan. Didn't want to add to his stress. It was already Christmas Eve and a fresh start was approaching. I remember spending the night at my Grandma's house preparing for Christmas dinner that year. For Jamaicans, Christmas is more than turkey and hot chocolate while you unwrap your presents. It's a huge party and preparations are exhausting. I was sound after a marathon of cooking and baking when one of my aunties came in to wake me up.

It was the middle of the night and I could tell by the tone of her voice something was wrong. The house was dark and quiet. She led me downstairs to where the foyer lit up, flooding my sleep-filled eyes with the brighter lights of the den. We walked through the adjoining living room where I got an eerie glimpse of almost every female member of my family waiting for me. They all had grim looks on their faces. I was scared and confused by their presence. It was my family and the in-laws all mixed together. The majority of them hated each other and never got along, especially at this time of year. I wondered what force could have brought them together.

I zoomed in on my own mother. Her eyes were blood shot and her Kleenex couldn't hold another tear. She called me over to where she was sitting, held my hands tightly, and struggled to say, "I have to tell you something".

I was really scared now. My mind kept screaming what? What is it? Tell me? But I kept my composure because Jamaicans are also known to be very dramatic. It might not be as bad as I thought.

But then she says, "Its Charles baby...they shot Charles"

It was as bad as I thought.

In that moment I didn't care about the who's, the when's, or the why's. I'm just like, "Well where is he? Which hospital is he at? Take me to him now! I want to see him!"

But she just kept shaking her head no. No. No. No. Like I didn't understand what she was saying.

I really didn't understand.

"He's dead baby. They shot Charles and now your father is dead".

◊

I guess I forgot to mention the hustler I was in love with wasn't just some man I met in the streets, buying me shit, and promising me the world. He was my father-the first man that ever loved me and the first man I ever loved. He was there the day I took my first breath and I was there the day he took his last. That day changed me. Changed my life forever.

It's so hard for me even now, 22 years later, to tell you what it was like to see my father lying in a coffin. How hard it was to grow up without him being there. The years of depression that plagued the remainder of my childhood and teenage years. Just knowing he never got to see me graduate; walk me down the aisle; or meet his grandchildren hurts my heart every day. There are no words that can really describe how difficult it was to go from being the princess of a drug empire to seeing my own grief stricken mother become a drug addict herself.

You see…the hustle killed both my parents that night. So I know both sides of the game. I saw the victims and became a victim myself.

That's why I'm warning all you sistahs out there. If you love a man that hustles, really love this man; not all the shit he can buy you, not the cars and the clothes, or the easy lifestyle; but who he really is as a person, help him get out.

Selling drugs can only lead to three things: jail, mental institutions, and death. The brothers that don't see the game changing always get locked up. The brothers that don't accept the game changing end up as addicts themselves. And the brothers that refuse to get out of the game before their time is up end up dead.

If you truly love this brother, help him get out before he strikes out. Encourage him to wash his money like the white folks do. You think white folks don't sell drugs? They might not be standing on the corners like we do, but they have their hand in the pot too. Tell your man to invest in something legit, like a business. Nag, nag, nag him until he listens. You have good credit? Good. Help him get some too. If you don't, go to school and get a job so you can build some. Beg your family members or friends with good credit to get ya'll the financing you need to go legit. 'Cause that's some other shit that forces black people to commit crimes: "No credit here" (it's not just a sign in the bodega). You walk into a bank and try to get a loan to open a legitimate business and they turn you down cold. You don't have any credit and you don't have any collateral. Sorry black man.

But maybe if we had got our 40 acres and a mule we wouldn't need your loan Mr. Chase. Maybe if we had got our reparations we wouldn't be crammed in the projects waiting on the 1st and the 15th Mr. Banks of America. And maybe, just maybe if this government didn't stop us from repatriating back to Africa when it finally decided to end slavery we'd be the CEOs of De Beers and all the other white owned companies still making billions off the mother land.

And let me tell you something else. The Jews use to be gangsters too. Both the Italian and Jewish Mafias capitalized on murder, racketeering, the sale of narcotics, and other organized criminal activities to make it in this country. But they learned to wash that dirty money until it got sparkling clean. Now their whole shit is legit. They live in affluent neighborhoods with each other and send their kids to the best schools in the country. Why not us? Why not you?

I'd go so far as to say if your man won't start a legit business on his own, start one for him. Open a little salon or a grocery store. Show him it can work. Convince him that with his hustler mentality and street smarts, you guys will be millionaires in no time. He'll believe it if you do. All a man ever really needs is his woman to have faith in him.

A LOOK IN THE MIRROR

Unfortunately not all sistahs in relationships with a hustler love his ass. When you love a man that hustles, you're going nuts when he doesn't answer his phone. You're worried about him being locked up? Robbed? Or laid up shot somewhere? You can't wait for him to walk safely through the front door so you can flip on him for worrying you so bad.

The sistahs that have no love for these men could care less how he makes his money (as long as he keeps making it). They're the gold digging women all men fear. They don't care if he's risking life and limb. They don't care what happens to him. Whether he sells drugs, raps, or plays ball, all they care about is how much money they can get to go shopping.

My advice to all the sistahs out there dating black men that hustle is to take a look in the mirror and figure out which one you are. Life is energy. You get what you give to the universe. Are you willing to do time for this man? Or will you be the first one to snitch him out when the feds coming knocking?

If you're a down ass chick, you both have my prayers. But if you're one of those women out there busy digging for gold, be careful not to bury yourself in the debris. It's not worth it.

Chapter 6

How to love a Black Man when…He's a Jailbird

"Love costs all we are and will ever be. Yet it is only love which sets us free."-Maya Angelou

There was a time when all black men were lynched for their crimes. If they were hungry and took a piece of bread, they were lynched. If they tried to escape from the plantation, they were lynched. If they looked at a white woman, they were lynched. No judge, no jury; just a good ole fashion lynching. And you know how white folks do. They go the extra mile to get their point across. They didn't just hang you from a tree and let you die in peace. First they would whip you good, tearing the flesh off your back. Then they would tie you behind the back of a buggy and drag you through the street. They invited all their friends and neighbors to come watch the "nigger swing". And just when you felt the last bit of life leaving your body, they would set you on fire and watch you burn. Some of them even took pictures of you as memorabilia and sent copies to their relatives as postcards.

I guess the current penal system is a better alternative to the latter. At least now you get some kind of trial before you are sentenced and sent back to the plantation. However policies like "probable cause" still lead to too many innocent black men being shot to death while walking to their cars after a bachelor's party; or getting beat over the head 53 times at a routine traffic stop; or being shot 41 times while attempting to open their front doors after a long day of work.

I live in a community that is 90% black, yet 90% of our police force is white. So when these so-called law enforcers come from their suburban, middle-class neighborhoods to our urban, inner-city hood, you don't hear them saying "how can I help you sir?" or "how can I assist you ma'am?" It's more like "hands up nigger" or "get down on the ground". They drive around more like the over-seers from the plantation than the peace officers our tax dollars are paying for. They harass and arrest us. Criminalize and victimize our people. I can't tell you how many times I've been driving home from work and seen my brothers lined up in the street, like slaves on the auction block, being frisked and searched for no reason at all.

As black people, we have to know our rights in order to survive an encounter with the police. For one thing, we have a right to be treated like citizens, not criminals when we are approached by the police for whatever reason, especially in our own communities. We have a right to ask questions like "am I being arrested and why?" We have a right to expect warrants before having our personal property and possessions searched. We have a right to be treated with respect. Unfortunately, it's still a challenge for black people to exercise these rights and many, many brothers are in jail as a result of that injustice.

So how do you love a black man who is locked up now or constantly in and out of jail AKA a jailbird? First let me clarify a couple of things. Not every brother in jail is a bad person. That's still somebody's son; somebody's brother; somebody's husband or father. Somebody has shed tears for what these brothers have done and all they've failed to do. Often our brothers (and some sistahs too) are put in positions where they make bad choices. But they still deserve some love and understanding; second chances and forgiveness despite their crimes.

Secondly, if your man was hustling and you benefited from his illegal activities... your ass better be there every visit day looking good and smelling better, don't forget he'll needs lots of reassurance that you love him and will be there for him when he gets home, and make sure you have your cell with you at all times to accept his calls (there are several ways to reduce the cost of collect calls; feel free to contact me and I'll fill you in). He's going to need money for his commissary and lots of love letters to read before he goes to bed at night. Don't let word get back to him you were messing with such 'n such from around the way and don't be out here acting like a fool. Unless your man says to you, "Don't wait for me, live your life", you better stand by your man.

If however, you're home one day, just chillin; the phone rings and when you pick it up you have an unexpected collect call from and inmate at whatever correctional facility; it's "Shawn" whom you haven't seen or heard from in over a year, don't accept the call. When you and "Shawn" dated before he got locked up he totally dogged you out and never appreciated you. Now that he's in the penitentiary he's experiencing a phenomenon I like to call "pen-i-therapy". Pen-i-therapy is what happens to black men whenever they are locked up and their world is no bigger than a 6x8 cell. They suddenly have all these epiphanies about life; including how much they need to change; and that you were always the one. It's not all their fault. Poverty and a failing educational system make it hard for black men to avoid the criminal activities that land them in jail in the first place. Violence is all they know. Then when they get out, their records prevent them from getting jobs, so they commit more crimes, and end up back in jail. It's a vicious cycle.

Now if "Shawn" happens to call back again, it's one of two things. Either no one else will accept his calls or he's in a really bad place and needs some love from the outside. Accept the call. Talk to him. Be his friend. Let him know what's new on the block and that he is missed. Promise to pray for him and keep that promise.

By no means are you to start a romantic relationship with him over some phone call from jail. Don't do it to yourself girl. This very same man will come home, taste freedom, and shit on you. It won't matter that he ran up your phone bill with collect calls or that you were there every visit day; that you sent him money and care packages; or that he promised you he was a changed man. Don't fall for it. He will shit on you.

When "Shawn" does come home, see where his head is at before you even think about having a relationship with him. Talk is cheap. People can change but only his actions and behavior will show you if he's a changed man or not. Maybe that last time he went in was the last time and he just needs someone to believe in him. Or maybe he'll go right back to his old ways. Either way, you need to be careful about the choices you make and the men you choose to share your life with. Thousands of sistahs are dying of AIDS right now because their man contracted the disease while he was in jail subsequently infecting her. Thousands of sistahs are the victims of domestic abuse because their man was in jail and came home more violent than he was when he went in. Please be careful my sistahs. It's your one precious life. Think about your futures. Think about your children.

A LOOK IN THE MIRROR

I know many women whom start and maintain relationships with brothers while they are still locked up. Some women even marry brothers in jail. Then when that same brother comes home, she makes him the man of her house, helps him get on his feet, has him feeling like somebody, and what does he do? Shit on her. These sistahs end up used, abused, and left alone by these brothers. This is when love hurts.

Jail does not rehabilitate our men. There is no rehabilitation or "correction" in the American prison system for the black man. The only thing our men learn while imprisoned is how to become better criminals, how to hate themselves, and how to hate each other. So-called "correction" officers treat our brothers like less than human throughout their incarcerations (slavery); our men are feed unhealthy, processed foods that have no nutritional value (slavery); they work for 10 or 15 cents an hour (slavery); and no matter how small their crimes they are mixed in with immoral men that rape and punk them, sending them home as "down-low brothers" and "homo-thugs" that spread disease to the sistahs at home waiting for them (more slavery). Once they are home the fear and burden of re-imprisonment, along with a lack of opportunities, can make our brothers their worst selves. It's literally a catch-22.

When our brothers do come home they need our love and support. As a community, we need to show them that love. We need more re-entry programs with concrete ways to help our brothers turn their lives around and avoid recidivism. We need more work programs and black owned business that will employ these brothers and not discriminate against them based on their records. We need to help our brothers understand and appreciate the importance of a man's liberty in this world. Only strong sistahs and a strong community can show him that.

When your man comes home, if all he can get is a minimum wage job at a fast food restaurant, show him how proud you are that he's going out and doing the right thing every day. Respect each penny he contributes to the home. Don't emasculate him or devalue his worth in this world. Pull the weight until he can do better. A good black woman can "correct" a brother better than any prison, any government program, or system in America can.

And when I called the brothers that repeatedly end up in jail "jailbirds" I wasn't trying to dis them. If you think about it, these brothers are like caged birds. If you open the cage and they fly away, they may never return. If however they do go back to that cage, they belong to the penal system for life.

Keep in mind there will never be enough "government funding" to improve the conditions in the black community. The little we get for our schools and housing is being cut by the government now. There is however, always enough funding to build new jails. They're building jails for our sons and daughters right now. I heard a statistic the other day that said 1 out of every 3 African-American boys that are now 10 years old is expected to be incarcerated by their 18th birthday with their chances doubled if their fathers have served any time. One out of three!

My hope is that more and more little black boys and girls will be sitting in criminal justice and law classes preparing to serve and protect our neighborhoods instead of being arrested in them. My hope is that more and more fathers will be home to steer their sons away from that path of criminalization and self-destruction instead of wasting away in a cell. My hope is for a better future for our people.

Only we can change the circumstances in our communities. Only we can change the futures of our children. Together, I hope we find a solution.

Peace.

Chapter 7

How to Love a Black Man, when…he's a Homosexual or

Down Low Brother

"Men are not women, and a man's balance depends on the weight he carries between his legs."-James Baldwin

The truth is an offense, not a sin. So I'm just gonna say what I gotta say and whoever don't like it can turn the page.

I want you to open your Afrikan mind right now. Think back to when we were our free and natural selves. Not enslaved and living under the influence of "Massa"; not unsegregated and living under the fear of Jim Crow; not a people granted human rights by the whim of some government after 400 years; just our free, natural, Afrikan selves.

So what does that really mean? It means there was nature and we took what was needed from the Earth, always considering the next generation, gave thanks, and kept it moving. There was order, meaning we respected our elders and sought their advice on family and village matters, gave thanks, and kept it moving. And there was family, meaning a man and a woman lived as equals, he being the head of the home, and she being the heart. I was not more important than him because I farmed and tended to the children and he was not more important than me because he hunted and protected the village. We lived a balanced harmony, gave thanks, and kept it moving.

So now that you remember who you are- a spiritual people- listen up!

Homosexuality is a sin. It's a sin against your body. It's a sin against your Afrikan soul. It's a sin against your ancestors and the future generations of black people. Period.

Nowhere...let us repeat that...nowhere. Not in our Afrikan history, not in our Afrikan cultures, not in our Afrikan art or folklores, not anywhere in our Afrikan selves was there any form or idea of homosexuality. There weren't even any words for homosexuality in any of our Afrikan languages because the behavior did not exist! Don't believe me, do your own research. When ya'll turn on your televisions if Dr. Whoever tells you the sky is purple you believe him/her without question despite the fact that white people have been lying to us for years! Now I'm no doctor of anything. I'm just your sistah speaking to you from love. But if you don't believe what I'm saying read the Isis Papers by Dr. Frances Cress Welsing, Homosexuality and the Effeminization of Afrikan Males by Mwalmu K. Bomani Baruti, The Conspiracy to Destroy Black Women by Michael Porter, Willie Lynch and the Making of a Slave, or the countless other books and research papers done by our own doctors that may never get a hit television show. Let your own brothers and sistahs tell you about whom you really are instead of believing in fairytales.

When I was a kid, I had no clue what homosexuality was. Everyone I knew or saw had relationships with the opposite sex. Furthermore, everyone I knew or saw, except for the nuns in my catholic school, were black. I thought men like Boy George and Liberace were weird. I had heard something about a famous white actor dying of AIDS and everyone saying he got it from being a homosexual. But that was television. It wasn't real to me. I remember watching sitcoms as a child and seeing two beds in the parents' room as though a married couple should not be having sex. Yet now when I turn on my television, on almost every show, all I see is homosexual behavior. There are homosexual characters kissing and having sex. There are homosexual characters getting married and having children. There are even homosexual cartoon characters subliminally influencing our children! Forget about reality television shows. These programs have really opened my eyes to the moral condition of this world.

Case in point, I have always wanted to move to or at least visit Atlanta, Georgia. Atlanta is the like the "Black Mecca" so to speak. Lots of famous athletes and entertainers live there. It's a place where black people live affluent lives and have entrepreneurial opportunities not found all over this country. So when a now very popular reality show about Atlanta aired on TV, I was an instant fan. It was one of my favorite guilty pleasures. But the more I watched the show, not only was I shocked to hear these so-called affluent black women calling each other "bitch" at the drop of a dime, I was extremely disappointed to see the number of homosexual black men in the city. And it wasn't just their numbers. It was their over the top and flamboyant behavior that really alarmed me. I'm talking black men- brothers- walking around in high heels, tight jeans, and makeup. Every other word for them too is "bitch" this and "bitch" that. I'm just like, are you serious? What are these guys trying to prove exactly? That they can be a woman? Better than women? And which sistahs are they imitating anyway. 'Cause no sistah I call a sistah even on her flyest day behaves that way. Our femininity comes from within. We don't have to try.

And why is this behavior being supported by the women on the show and in our communities? Ever hear it takes a village to raise a child? Where is the village now to stand up and say "brother you're living foul"? I know they're wonderful hairstylists and fashion gurus. Only "Antoine" can cut your hair, right? Only "Dre" can style you for your next premier event. But let's get real here. Men are by nature visual creatures. Of course they know what looks good on a woman. Some of my favorite outfits were picked out and purchased for me by my husband. Of course a man can style a woman's hair. Men are skilled with their hands. Look at some of the great architecture men have created in this world. Most of the great chefs in the world are men. Do you really need high heels and dick in your ass to do that? Are we sistahs as culpable for supporting them? I'm sure if the line at "Antoine's" beauty shop wasn't out the door, he couldn't afford those Prada heels he's prancing around in. Real brothers don't wear high heels. Brothers have natural style and swag. They can make sweats and a t-shirt look good. I'm also certain if "Dre" wasn't surrounded by black women calling each other "bitch" all day, it wouldn't be so easy for him to think he could imitate the royalty true black women possess.

Now let's talk the facts. No, better yet, let's talk sex first. Cause let's face it, homosexual behavior is about sex. Call it what you like, gay, homosexual, bisexual, lesbian, MSM (Men who have sex with men), WSW (Women who have sex with women), it's all about sex. So let's talk about it.

So a man has a sex gland in his anus, the prostate, right? So let's deal with the prostate. The prostate is an important part of a man's reproductive system. True. But

God didn't put it there for the so called "anal orgasm". The prostate functions almost like a spa treatment for a man's sperm. It provides fluids and nutrients that protect the sperm and keep it healthy and strong to increase the chances of it fertilizing an egg. It makes vitamins and enzymes that help the sperm swim through and survive in the vagina (FYI sperm can live in the vagina for up to three days) to ensure it finds an egg and makes a baby. The prostate also causes the uterus to contract (female orgasm) and it also contracts when a man ejaculates to prevent urine from being released into the semen (so-called anal orgasm). The same mechanism that connects our breasts to our uterus; which is the reason why if a man kisses our breasts we feel a tingle all over our bodies or why when we breastfeed our babies we feel the pull way down in our abdomens is the same mechanism that connects a man's prostate to his penis. It's just the way the things works. Do ya'll think God was playing around when he designed the human body?

There is no machine, no car, no computer, no man-made anything as efficient as or as beautiful as the human body. We have pumps, and systems, and electrical circuits in our bodies unmatched by any machine. The human body can heal and repair itself when injured. If you treat your body right, eat well and exercise, you can run, jump, swim, and climb better than any creature on this planet. So if God took the time to make us such perfect and efficient beings, why are we telling HIM he's wrong? Men and women fit together like pieces of a puzzle, perfect matches that can create the perfect picture. Yet gay men are forcing their penises into each other's anuses. And keep in mind, whether it holds the prostate or not, the anus is a filthy place. It's the part our body's that holds and expels the body's garbage… feces. It's filled with bacteria. The tearing, bleeding, and damage to the muscles of the anus that occur during homosexual/anal sex is a breeding ground for a number of diseases including all the Hepatitis's, AB, and C, HPV, and the worst killer of them all, HIV. And if you ever wondered why gay men have such a "feminine" walk, let me clarify there is nothing feminine about it. Repeated anal sex causes anal prolapse, which means the actual rectum will begin to protrude outside of their buttholes. They walk like that, switching their hips with clenched butt-cheeks, not because it's feminine, but because they gotta keep their shit in. And that's real talk.

Just the other night I was watching Taxicab Confessions on HBO and there was a transsexual passenger in the taxi describing that many of his/her transsexual friends became "crazy" after they "got the pussy"; that many transsexual men were depressed and suicidal after cutting off their penises for a man-made vagina; and for that reason, he/she (the passenger in the taxi) would not be getting the surgery, but would continue to live and dress as a woman. So basically all these homosexual and transsexual brothers are telling us sistahs even though we have all this sweet, warm, juicy pussy waiting right here for them; all this big booty, bouncy breasts, and soft skin; their choice of dark chocolate, milk chocolate, caramel, or latte; they would rather stick their dicks in the toilet? They would rather dress up as women themselves? Brother please. Ya'll need to stop trying so hard to be "gentle-men" and just get back to being the men God created you to be.

As for all the sistahs whom call themselves lesbians. Do some research on the origin of the word? Lezbo was a small European island for exiled prostitutes known for giving the best blow jobs. And I don't care what kind of toys they buy or how well they can lick each other, there is still nothing like a brother putting it on your ass. And that's real talk too.

Funny that our sex organs and their functions are classified under the Reproductive System, meaning to reproduce. Yet two men or two women cannot naturally produce a child together. I'm just saying.

Then they say it's not about sex. It's not about reproduction. Okay fine. Let's say some gay couples aren't even having sex (all though sex is as basic a human need as food and water). Let's say some people engage in homosexual or gay relationships for the companionship and so called compatibility of being with the same sex.

Are you for real? Of course you get along well with you bros or male friends. Men understand you don't talk about your feelings during the last minute of the game. Men know after a hard day of work you just want to sit quietly and drink a beer. That's called brotherhood. Only a man can show a man how to be a man. Which is why in Afrikan societies, our boys are initiated by the elder men on how to be men: preparing for marriage and fatherhood, how to defend his home, and other rites of passage to teach the boys morality and social responsibility. And of course we ladies have our BFFs and our female friends we just couldn't live without. Our girls understand everything we are going through; they understand our cramps and pms. Of course we can shop and talk to them for hours about nothing. That's what women do! It's called sisterhood. Only a woman can teach a woman how to be a woman. My grandmother taught me how to cook and clean the house. My mother showed me how to comb my hair, to put on my first pad, and later to take care of my first baby. In Afrikan societies a rite of passage for our girls is to spend time with the elder women preparing for motherhood and marriage. Does that mean we should all be having sex with each other because we get along so well?

Afrikan love- black love- is about compatibility. Men and women balance each other. We complement each other. As much as the gay community argues that gay relationships are the same as straight relationships, really they are not. Maybe the fact that there is no issue of gender roles in their home life provide gay couples with a certain level of peace. They both do the dishes; they both take out the garbage, etc. But peace is something we should all strive for, a challenge to keep life balanced. With two men or two women, where is the balance in that? Ever hear of opposites attracting; the ying and the yang in life?

Furthermore, being in a same sex relationship does not guarantee continuous peace. When two men disagree, and things get heated, whether they are gay or straight, better believe it will lead to a physical confrontation. And if you didn't know one thing about homosexual men, know this; gay domestic violence between two men is worse than any domestic violence between a man and a woman because those two men may beat each other to a bloody pulp.

Two gay women may seem to have the best of both worlds, basically having an intimate relationship with their best friend, but where is the balance when conflict does arise? Sure they may be able to keep the lines of communication open without any physical confrontation. Women love to talk about our feelings. That's what we do. We can go from emotion to emotion with no logical end. Not saying we can't be logical about relationship issues. But women are by nature very emotional creatures, especially when it comes to our relationships and loved ones. So again, where is the balance? Where is the challenge?

Real brothers want to solve our problems. Not just talk about them. They want to protect us. They want to provide for us. And real sistahs make their men listen when they need to. We show our men how to be loving fathers and good husbands. We motivate them to fulfill their destinies...to be great men. It's a delicate balance. It's a beautiful thing. The natural balance between a man and a woman also explains why so many gay men have female best friends or "fag-hags". Men and women need each other.

The reason black relationships are in such turmoil and why we suddenly have this explosion of homosexual behavior in the black community is because, sorry to say, we're acting like white folks.

Open your logical minds and take a look at how white folks live. Think back to all the required European and white history you were forced to study in school as a child. Look at their lifestyle, their ideals, even their mythology.

Now that you remember who we're dealing with, let us with hears ear and those with eyes see...

Homosexuality is a white man's problem. It is a white man's dilemma. They've been practicing it for years. The Europeans concealed their homosexual practices from black people because they knew we would find it unacceptable. Unfortunately, like many white behaviors, Afrikan people have now assimilated this behavior. Period.

I find it amazing that black people, without question, continue to believe the lies white people tell us. When they told us we were slaves we became slaves, when they told us we were niggers, we became niggers, now they tell us to be gay, so we're gay. When have white people ever meant any good for us or told us the truth about anything unless it benefited them? Listen, I'm no racist. I'm not saying all white people are evil. I have white in-laws and half white relatives. I have gone to school with and worked with some really cool white people. Like I tell my children, there were white abolitionists that tried to help us while we were enslaved. And now because of Hip-Hop and Hip-Hop culture, white people are completely enamored with us. They always have been. They listen to our music; they dress like us; they talk like us. As we speak there are white people tanning their skin to the point of getting skin cancer just to be "colored". White women are getting butt implants and lip implants to look more "exotic". Today's white people don't even see your race as long as the economics are right. Just ask OJ or Tiger! So why do we continue to try and fit in with them and imitate their ways when they have always been trying to imitate us?

I'm not even saying all white people are gay; but they do have tendencies. White college girls are always kissing on each other and "experimenting" with same sex relationships. White men like to explore their feminine side and have "metrosexual" rituals. Frankly, white people do a lot of weird shit I don't understand like going outside in the middle of winter wearing shorts; bungee jumping; enslaving other human beings all over the world based on the color of their skin; you know, shit like that. Homosexuality is just another strange thing they do, and in the black community, it's another example of us trying to be white. Everything's all right as long as you're trying to be white. White people feel more comfortable by our presence in society the further we stray from our Afrikan selves. What I don't understand is why do we still care about the comfort level of white people? What more do we owe them?

When the white man landed on the shores of Africa in the name of "exploration", he didn't say, "listen here folks, after you teach us how to survive on your land we're going to steal the land from you, claim it as our own, rob it of every ounce of diamonds and gold we can get our hands on, separate you from your families, throw you in the bottom of a ship, and bring you to the other side of the planet so you can be our slaves and make us rich. Then after about 400 years of torturous beatings, whippings, and other inhumane living conditions, we'll set you free. But we're going to make laws to keep you separated from us, lynch you at will, and pay you minimum wage for the same work you used to do for free. Then after another 50 years of that, we'll murder all your Malcoms, and your Medgars and your Martins; hose you down in the streets and sick our dogs on you. Then when we're good and ready, we'll grant you some civil rights, throw you in the projects, make sure there is a liquor store on every corner, and enough crack and heron in the streets for everyone. Sound good to you?"

They didn't tell us that, right? So you think they were going to add, "Oh and by the way, even though you guys seem like some real spiritual and very family oriented people, we white men really like having sex with each other, especially with our teenage sons. We'll start out by raping your woman for a while, but eventually we'll move onto your sons too."

It never bothers me when I see a white man or white woman engaged in homosexual behaviors or relationships. To me, they are just being themselves. But when I see my own brothers or sistahs carrying themselves in that way, I truly feel embarrassed. Doesn't matter if you're African, African-American, Latino, or Hispanic; we all share African blood. My brother's shame is my own.

So let's talk more facts. We don't have time to discuss the openly homosexual relationships that Socrates, Alexander the Great, Julius Cesar, Michelangelo, and other historically significant white men practiced long before they ever reached the shores of Africa. And we really don't have time to break down the white man's preoccupation and obsession with phallic symbols; the homosexual aspects of Europe's so-called great works of art; or even the fact that their great Greek gods, like Zeus, all had male lovers. That would be a whole other book and you will have to do that research on your own.

I will however mention that the slang term for anal sex among Europeans is called "doing it the Greek way" and I also want you to consider this:

1. Greeks and Romans alike practiced a rite of passage with their sons called pederasty. Unlike the rites of passage practiced amongst Afrikan societies that are geared towards initiating our souls through birth, adulthood, marriage, and our ancestry; pederasty is a sexual relationship between an older man and a boy, preferably a teenage boy. It literally means to love boys or to love children. It was considered not only an important initiation into their societies, but also a requirement to join the military. Funny how the root and meaning of the word pederasty is similar to pedophile. Why do

you think white men loved to refer to our black men as "boys; come here boy; do this boy, do that boy"? They're "boy lovers". They've been trying to effeminize black men for centuries. I'm sure they are happy to see black men now prancing around in heels. It makes them feel more comfortable with the black man's presence in this world. They don't have to worry about the Zulu or Mau Mau spirits rising up against them anymore.

2. According to the Department of Justice website there are over 4 million registered pedophiles and child molesters in this country. The average pedophile usually has at least 75 victims before he his caught.

    a. Are you telling me all these sick, perverted men out there; touching little boys and girls, have no effect on the future of these children's sexuality? Are you telling me that these "lovers of children" aren't the same scout leaders we entrust our children to go off camping with? The same priests accused of molesting all those altar boys? Are you telling me this has no influence on the number of homosexual people in the world "out of the closet" today? C'mon people, do the math.

3. They're building jails for our brothers every day. There are some places in this

country where working at the jail/prison is the main source of income for everybody that lives in that town. It's a separate economy for that state. So-called "correctional facilities" are big business; big politics. Ever heard of the Rockefeller Laws?

    a. So with half our brothers locked up for maybe robbing someone, selling a little dope, or some other what I like to call "crimes of survival"-not good, not condoning it, but it is what it is. You're telling me that this criminalization and over-exposure of our brothers to all the white serial killers, rapists, pedophiles, and sodomites have nothing to do with the explosion of homosexual behavior in the black community? The advent of the "homo-thug", the "down-low brothers" and MSMs?

And last but certainly not least...

4. Black men love pussy. They pride themselves on how much they can get, how they handle it when they get it, and despite the fact that it sits between your legs...that it's their pussy. Black people are the only people that were able to continuously reproduce while in captivity. The Native Americans completely shut down and stop making babies when the

> Europeans enslaved them. They refused to
> make more slaves. But not us. Despite
> being tortured and beaten on a daily basis,
> we still turned to each other for love and
> support; we kept on fucking and produced
> millions of slaves and billions of dollars
> for the white folks in this country.

As I explained before, homosexuality in the black
community is an assimilated behavior. Assimilation helps
everybody get along. It makes the ruling culture, the white
culture, feel more at ease by our presence because we are
adapting to their ways. And even though we might finally
have a black president and a few of us are making millions,
let's face it, white people still run this country. They made
slavery legal. They made segregation legal. And now they're
making gay marriage legal as well. White people make
anything pro-white right despite the moral implications;
that's just how they are. As far as I know black people are
too busy trying to survive life in the hood to worry about gay
rights. We're too busy fighting for funding for our schools,
for housing, and trying to keep our black assess out of jail.
We just got our own rights 50 years ago! To add insult to
injury, the "gay rights movement" is now being compared to
the Civil Rights Movement. Black people were treated like
less than human: enslaved, beat, lynched, and hosed down in
the streets just for being black; and now that compares to
people who choose to take dick up their ass. This country is
unbelievable.

And if you still don't think homosexuality is a white
behavior, why is it that homosexual white men and women
are flourishing in this new "gay world". Why do they have so

much influence and power in their communities and in politics? Why is there so much acceptance and such a strong push for gay marriage and legislation to protect gay rights?

So since I'm not a racist, I guess you would call me homophobic. But you're wrong about that too. Black people and the black community have always been accused of being homophobic. But let me make it clear, I have no irrational fear or phobias when it comes to homosexuals. I actually feel sorry for them. I am by trade a nurse and worked in an AIDS hospice for many years. I took care of a lot of gay men that experienced many of the medical problems that I mentioned before. I've had gay classmates and worked with lots of cool gay people (and trust me, I've had serious conversations with them about sex and their relationships and didn't hesitate to ask them the things I always wanted to know). I see people, all people, as children of God. It's their behavior I disagree with. It's having to explain to my 9 year old the difference between bisexuals and homosexuals; or how it's possible for two men to have a baby when I already told him daddies put the babies in a mommy's belly; or just the look of confusion on his face when he sees two guys kissing at the mall or two girls holding hands in the park.

I wonder now if homosexuality, not infertility, is the real reason Europeans created sperm banks and the whole process or sperm donation in the first place. Kind of like a backup plan to preserve their race while allowing them to indulge in their sexual "preferences". Everyone seems to thinks it's our carbon emissions and recyclables that are warming the globe. But ya'll better start paying attention to how our morality, or lack thereof, is contributing to the destruction of the planet as well.

If you really want to discuss someone having an irrational fear of homosexuals or questioning their homosexual tendencies, it's white men. It's been their dilemma in life, not ours. They are the ones that chose to introduce these practices and behaviors into their societies. It was their weakness; their shameful secret and fear of exposure that has caused all this madness. White people seem to love that domination-submission shit; one man sodomizing the other; shoving butt plugs and anal beads up each other's asses; women wearing strap-ons. Why would I want another woman to strap on a fake penis anyway when there are plenty of well-endowed brothers walking around with the real thing? That's what they call love making; a natural part of life?

And of course there is now scientific proof that homosexuality is genetic, it's DNA, "they are born that way". There used to be scientific proof that black people were inferior, that we were animals. White people can always come up with scientific proof when they want you to believe in something. So now there is scientific proof homosexuality is natural. Let's talk about that.

Whenever the gay community or other supporters of homosexuality say they are "born that way", what they're trying to imply is that God has a hand in this. God made them that way. But let me tell you something about my Heavenly Father the Creator, the Most High. Something you might not know: there is no way that God could be so wicked as to cause someone to be "born that way".

What human beings seem to forget is, not only did God give us the gift of life; he also gave us the gift of free will, the ability to make choices. Life is about the choices we make. Human beings also seem to forget that our actions, behaviors, and even environmental factors can change a person's cells; can change their DNA. Even if it doesn't affect them now, it may affect their off-spring; may even skip a generation before the problem shows up.

People aren't born with cancer. There may be some genetic predisposition to it that they got from their parents. But God didn't do that. God didn't create the stress people experience in their lives. God didn't create the pollution, radiation, insecticides or any of the other factors they say may cause cancer. God gave us a beautiful, clean, and peaceful Earth to live on. We're the ones that are destroying it.

When someone is addicted to drugs or alcohol, sure they may have a genetic predisposition to it because their mother or father was an alcoholic; it's now in their genes; it was in their environment. But it wasn't God that made them an alcoholic. God didn't make the alcohol or cause them to drink it. God doesn't make us drink or use drugs. I heard a very popular radio talk show host in New York use that very analogy when discussing homosexuality in the black community on a recent program. He said something like "saying people choose to be homosexual is like saying an addict chooses to be an addict". But like I just said, an addict may have been born with that predisposition; may have grown up in an environment where substances were abused; but you better believe every time they cash their checks or rob someone, and take that money to their dealer, they are making a choice. And every time they pick up that bottle to take a drink or pick up that crack pipe to take a hit, they are making a choice. And every day that they stay on the wagon; go to their AA/NA meetings; and do what the fuck they gotta do to stay sober, that's a choice they make too. So of course homosexuality may very well be in the genes or DNA of someone, but God didn't do that. That's their genetic defect. That's their choice.

And why would someone choose to be homosexual; choose to be ostracized; to possibly lose their family and friends? Because they're weak that's why. A homosexual man is too weak to balance a woman and a homosexual woman is too weak to balance a man. So they turn to each other. Period.

I also mentioned before the number of sex offenders and pedophiles registered and unregistered in this country. I'm not saying every homosexual person was traumatized, molested, or raped. White men have willingly practiced homosexuality for years. It should be no surprise to them if their sons or daughters turn out to be gay. What I'm saying to you is this…white/European homosexual behavior spread throughout the world during their "explorations" and was forced on us during slavery. They traumatized us! The influence of these "children lovers" not only led to homosexuality in our community, but to the trauma and homosexuality of our own children and their off-spring as well. Fortunately for us, we are a strong people and have conquered worse. As far as I'm concerned homosexuality in the black community is like the Jheri Curl; we thought it was cute, but now it's time to go natural.

But our question remains, how do you love a black man when he's a homosexual or even worse, a "down low brother"? Sistahs, the answer is prayer. We have to pray for these men. As I mentioned before we should not be supporting or endorsing their behavior. There are plenty of talented women out there that can cut your hair. And if you can afford a stylist, there are plenty of women who can shop for you and be your assistants. I'm not saying prayers will miraculously change the brothers who have been practicing homosexuality for years. It's not easy to get sugar out of a gas tank. Our prayers are for our children; the future generations of little black boys and girls growing up in this confused world.

If you discover you're in a relationship with what we call a "down-low brother", for the sake of your own health, the only answer is to end the relationship. Once you heal from the pain and hurt of being in a situation like that, then the prayers can begin. Pray for the brother, show him forgiveness, and share with him what you have learned in this book. Don't ostracize him. He needs sisterly love. He will have to come to terms with his behavior, its origins, and choose the lifestyle he feels is right for him on his own. 'Cause no matter whom or what you believe in, everyone gets their judgment day.

A LOOK IN THE MIRROR

I want to specifically address my single black mother's out there. Before I got married, I was raising my eldest son alone. Playing mother and father to a child is a challenge I could never imagine and believe me I feel your pain. I'm not saying a woman cannot raise her son to be a man by herself. We've done it, we do it, and many of us will continue to do it because unfortunately a lot of brothers are not living up to their responsibilities as fathers, as men. What I want to say to you is this. Even though you are the head of the house, large and in charge, don't effeminize your sons. Keep in mind that he may be just a boy now, but one day he will be a man. He doesn't need to hear you bash his father or every man that has done you wrong. He doesn't need to sit in the salon for eight hours listening to women gossip while you get your weave done. He doesn't need to watch the new episode of America's Next Top Model with you. He's a man. Be sure he has a positive black man in his life to be his jegna and raise him to be a man.

We Afrikans thrive on spirituality and respect for each other. We respect our elders because they are our past and we respect our children because they are our future. Treat your sons with respect. Discipline him, be firm when you need to; but talk to him and treat him with respect. I'm appalled when I hear black women call their children "little motherfuckers" or "stupid asses" while disciplining their children in the street; or when describing how irritated they are by their own children. If you think that about your own child, how will the rest of the world see him? How will he see himself? If you treat your sons with respect they will respect you back. Always remember your son will be a man one day and technically you are his first woman.

Oh, and one other thing. Don't be walking around your sons, especially as they approach their pre-teen and teenage years with your boobies and asses hanging out. I'm not saying you have to start dressing like Big Mama. But at least cover up when you're not fully dressed. Put on a robe for God's sake! Your son is becoming a man. He's discovering his own sexuality; getting little hard-ons and having wet dreams. He doesn't need to see his mother's butt cheeks hanging out of her boy-cut shorts while she's cooking dinner or her thong sticking out of her jeans every time she bends over. Nudity is natural. Of course our children will see us naked at one time or another. But do you really want your son developing an oedipal complex or being totally confused about his sexuality because he equates sexiness with his mother? Those are just more white man dilemmas. Our sons don't need that. Stop trying so hard to be a M-I-L-F and just be a mom.

And when you're raising your daughters on your own she doesn't need to hear that "all men ain't shit". You don't need to bash her father. You shouldn't let her see a parade of men coming through your house either. She's going to be a woman one day. You should want her to experience having a man in her life that truly loves her, especially if she didn't get that love from the first man that should have given it to her, her father. She needs that love from you too so she doesn't think she has to get it from some other woman.

◊

A few months ago in the news, three children committed suicide because they were supposedly homosexual and had been bullied by their peers or perhaps just confused and depressed by their feelings. I can't say for sure. But I said to myself…what are we doing to our children? Instead of protecting their innocence, this society has saturated their brains and lives with homosexuality, leaving them in a state of confusion. Confusion so bad the only solution they could come up with was death. That's deep. I started thinking back to when I was just 12 or 13 years old and had a major crush on a boy in my class, the way he rejected me, and how it made me question if I was too unpopular, too shy, or just too ugly for any boy to like me. It wasn't the last time my heart was broken by a boy either. Then I wondered if I was a teenager now, and I turned on the TV, and saw all this homosexual behavior, would my adolescent brain convince me I should be a homosexual too? Would I decide right then and there all boys suck, girls are nicer to me anyway, so maybe I should just be gay too? Well guess what, all boys do suck when you're 13 and adolescent girls can be the meanest people on the planet. That's normal adolescent behavior.

Recently there was another controversial advertisement in the news. It was for J.Crew clothing featuring a white mother and her son with his toenails painted neon pink!? Can you imagine our sons running around the hood with neon pink toenails! What message is J.Crew trying to send to little boys? That it's okay to be feminine? It's okay to be gay?

In the eighties they started giving little boys dolls to play with instead of toy guns and trucks. Thirty years later all those little boys have grown up to be today's gay men. Now they want our sons to wear makeup. What's next?

It's truly a shameful world when parents don't take the job of parenting seriously. It's truly a shameful world when we won't even let children be children anymore. If white mothers want to polish their son's toenails, put them in beauty pageants, and let them play "dress-up" in their heels, let them. White folks have their way of living and we have our way. Live and let live. Just know yourself my brothers and sistahs. Know your history. Know your culture. Peace.

Chapter 8

How to Love a Black Man when...he's an Addict or Abusive

"There is always something to do. There are always hungry people to feed, naked people to clothe, sick people to comfort and make well. And while I don't expect you to save the world I do think it's not asking too much for you to love those with whom you sleep, share the happiness of those whom you call friend, engage those around you who are visionary, and remove from your life those who offer you depression, despair and disrespect."-Nikki Giovanni

I'm going to keep this one real simple. Millions of people have a glass of wine with dinner. Another million grab a beer after work. Clubs and bars are filled with people that go out every weekend and get totally wasted just for fun. But there is a difference between having fun and being addicted to drugs or alcohol.

Addiction is a serious dis-ease of the mind and body. It changes the way you live and function in your life. People that are addicted to drugs and alcohol have an uncontrollable need for that drug or alcohol despite the consequences to their personal and professional lives.

If you are addicted to drugs or alcohol put this book down right now, walk yourself into the emergency room and let them know you're trying to kill yourself and need help. They will admit you or send you to a psychiatric facility where you can detox and begin going to AA/NA meetings depending on your drug of choice. A social worker can get you into a 30, 60, or 90 Day program depending on your history and severity of your addiction. After that, it's up to you to change the people you hang out with, the places you go, and the things you consider fun, one day at a time.

If your man is addicted to drugs or alcohol you need to put this book down, take him to the emergency room, let them know he is trying to kill himself and needs help. They will admit him or send him to a psychiatric facility where he can detox and begin going to AA/NA meetings depending on his drug of choice and a social worker can refer him to a 30, 60, or 90 Day program depending on his history and severity of his addiction. When he comes home it's up to him to change the people he hangs out with, the places he goes, and the things he considers fun, one day at a time. Your role is to be his support system and understand his addiction. Don't enable his behavior by giving him money to support his habit. Don't call his job to say he's sick when he is high, has a hangover, or is MIA. Go to meetings with him. Take him to church with you. Be his support.

Black men often abuse drugs and alcohol due to the same poverty and lack of opportunities that causes a lot of them to end up in jail. They feel hopeless and helpless and use drugs to escape the reality of their lives. They're basically depressed and self-medicating and can't even see the real -ISMs behind it. Addiction is a long and difficult battle. You may make that trip to the emergency room several times. There will be relapses and return trips to rehab. Many people have to lose everything: their work, their homes, their friends, family, and relationships; even their physical and mental health before they hit "rock bottom" and decide to turn their lives around. You may have to do an intervention. You may have to break up with him and totally cut him off to keep your own sanity. Prayer will help you through.

◊

A man may become abusive towards his woman for different reasons. He may be insecure, he may need anger management, he may have his own history of abuse from his childhood, or maybe he just thinks respect comes from fear and control over his women. Abuse can come in several forms. It can be physical, mental, or emotional. Who feels it knows it. So if your man yells at you, puts you down, neglects you, beats you, rapes you, threatens you, or mistreats you in any way, LEAVE HIM. It will only get worse. I don't care how small in stature a man is; men have muscle mass and testosterone coursing through their veins that can outmatch even a very strong and muscular woman. You can lose your life or be seriously injured or disfigured by this man. Even if you're fighting back, why would you want to be with a man you have to fight? What's next? He pulls a gun on you, stabs you; sets you on fire? It's better to separate before you end up hurt and he ends up in jail. Black men are more likely to be sentenced to time for whatever crimes they commit; only white men walk out of court with probation and dismissals. It's a bad situation for the both of you. Get out now.

You should also keep in mind that a man that abuses you will also abuse your children. Promiscuous teen girls and run-aways are often the product of sexual and physical abuse inflicted on them by their mothers' boyfriends or husbands; early exposure to sexual experiences lead to over-sexed teenage girls that end up as teenage mothers. Boys that witness and experience domestic violence often mimic the same behavior in their own relationships and many, many boys are the silent victims of sexual abuse as well.

So don't keep abuse a secret. Tell your family and friends what's really going on. There are shelters and other services for battered women that can help you get out of this situation as well. If you don't speak up now, your abusive relationship may be a secret you literally take to the grave.

Men that abuse women need professional help and counseling. Their issues are deeper than you. He can change. But don't lose your life waiting for that to happen.

And if you're the abusive one...yelling and screaming in this man's face. As soon as you get angry about something here you go raising your hands to this man while he's trying to do the right thing by not knocking you out; go and get yourself some counseling and anger management too. No one deserves to be abused.

Chapter 9

How to Love a Black Man when…he's a Chauvinist

"Tell me whom you love, and I'll tell you who you are."-African-American Proverb

There's no better way for me to illustrate chauvinism in the black community other than Hip-Hop and Hip-Hop culture. First let me say I am a huge lover and supporter of Hip-Hop music. I have been listening to rap since I first heard Rapper's Delight. Will always have love for Eric B and Rakim; and totally down with the early Def Jam movement: Run-DMC, LL Cool J, The Beastie Boys. I've seen Crush Groove more times than I can count. My own children listen to Slick Rick the storyteller even now. And I still listen to Public Enemy and The X-Clan when I need black power.

When Grandmaster Flash said, "don't push me 'cause I'm close to the edge"; how many youth in the black community felt the same way? When Tupac said, "Even as a crack fiend, mama, you always was a black queen"; how many of us were dealing with a drug addicted parent we still loved and admired despite their flaws? When Biggie said he was "just trying to make enough money to feed my daughter"; how many brothers were in jail for trying to do the same thing? I remember case workers had my moms "runnin' back to face to face". And "in the summers, free lunch held *us* (like Ghostface) down like steel" too.

Music has always been a powerful force in the black community. The chant and beat of the Afrikan drum has always been in our hearts. We sent messages to each other in our "old negro spirituals" back on the plantation. We've protested apartheid and other human injustices peacefully through song. There was a time when our music wasn't even allowed on the radio unless it was covered by a white artist. Hip-Hop music gives today's black youth a chance to be heard. The struggles and hustle in our hoods; the dreams and aspirations of our people; even the latest dance moves are clearly expressed through the talents of these young people. They use their poetic and lyrical skills to tell the world how it really is. Rapper El General recently incited revolution amongst the youth in Egypt with his music. Hip-Hop is a global phenomenon and a powerful force to be reckoned with. It can't be stopped.

But Hip-Hop also has a dark side. It has become an exclusive boy's only club that has many songs that objectify and degrade black women and all women in general. The misogynistic lyrics and portrayal of half-naked, light skinned women in music videos is designed to create division amongst our people by the white record label and magazine owners that really control the industry. Yet another example of "Massa's" control over our communities.

The few women that make it in the industry must sell their own sexuality and objectify themselves to earn a living. How many Queen Latifahs, Sistah Souljahs, Erykah Badus, and Lauren Hills get spins on the radio today? How many underground sistahs with something to say do we ever hear on the radio? Even some R&B songstresses like Rihanna sing explicit sexual lyrics just to make a sale. Where are the Mary J. Bliges and Faiths; the Brandys and Monicas; the Hip-Hop soul sistahs that sing more about the soul and less about the sex when we really need them? All I hear over and over, no matter which station I switch to, is Nicki Minaj and her Barbies; Drake glorifying his love for strippers and calling women bitches and hoes; Kanye telling his women, "less talk, more head right now"; and Lil' Wayne blatantly describing his drug and sex escapades.

Why don't we hear more from rappers like Black Thought, Mos Def, and Talib Kweli; Dead Prez; the Lupe Fiascos and Commons out there? Damian and Nas had one of the greatest albums I ever heard last year yet they get no airplay. Rappers with something to say just don't get played on the radio; you don't see their videos repeatedly shown on MTV or BET either. Once again, a positive aspect of black culture has been victimized by white America in the name of the almighty dollar. So where does that leave us as a people?

Any rapper can say, "I'm not a role model; I just sing about my life; what I live; what I see". But to me, that's a cop out. When your music is being pumped into the community from every car that passes by; when we see you on TV in your videos, reality and award shows; when we're buying clothes, shoes, and other merchandise just because it has your name on it there has to be some level of responsibility on the part of the rapper. Like it or not rappers send a strong message to the teenagers and young adults growing up in the hood about how they should dress, speak, and interact with each other; especially when no other positive role model exist in their lives. Even if rappers claim to be singing about their own experiences, why glorify the negative aspects? Why not show the youth there is a better way for us to be?

There is no other genre of music where the men degrade their women the way Hip-Hop music degrades us sistahs. Hip-Hop is a gross display of sexism towards black women. You'll never hear a Country singer calling his woman a bitch or hoe. You'll never hear Rock-n-Roll musicians telling white women to "suck it or not". Sure they have their groupies and threesomes too; they often sing about falling in love or getting their hearts broken by a woman. But you will never hear them singing songs that violate their white sisters the way brothers sing songs that violate and humiliate us. White men keep white women and white womanhood on a pedestal. They know the difference between real life and entertainment. The problem is a lot of black people don't seem to overstand that difference and too many brothers out there believe in and emulate the things rappers say.

So how do you love a black man that is a chauvinist; a sexist brother that degrades and destroys black womanhood through his words, actions, and imitation of today's a rap icons because he thinks it's cool or manly? First let me say there will always be men that see women as inferior to them. They like their women sexy and brainless; pretty little things that decorate their masculine world. They see strippers, porn stars, and other women that use their bodies to make money or entertain men as the definition of a woman. If you have no problem with a man disrespecting and degrading you just because he thinks he can, more power to you. If you don't mind dropping it low; shaking it; or clapping it for the attention of a man and his money, get it girl! Just don't act surprised when after these men give you their money they call you a hoe, freak, skeezer, trick, chicken-head, jump-off, or bitch to your face and treat you as such.

The reality is these men are enjoying their lives and have no plans on turning any hoes into housewives. They will marry the "good-girls" when the time is right. So if you are one of the "good-girls" out there and have some dignity, pride, and respect for yourself, never stand for a brother (or any man for that matter) treating you in a disrespectful way. I don't care if he's your husband, father, brother, neighbor, or boss. I don't care how much he claims to love you. It is a woman's responsibility to carry herself in a manner that demands and commands respect. It is our responsibility to show our men (and all men) what Afrikan womanhood and sisterhood mean to us and to the future of our people as a whole.

There are so many women all over the world that have no rights, no choices, and no autonomy in their lives. They would be shot dead if they left their homes with their heads or faces uncovered. They are the victims of sexual abuse and violence by the hands of their own men. African-American and American women in general have more rights and freedoms than we know what to do with, forgetting there are sistahs around the world that don't have these same rights, yet still manage to hold themselves in a high regard. Always respect each other and always respect yourself.

Peace.

A LOOK IN THE MIRROR

Chauvinist men are considered old fashioned and uncompromising to a fault. It seems as though these men missed the whole point of the Women's Right and Women's Lib movements. Today's woman doesn't want or need a man like that. But what I would like us to keep in mind is that no man wants or needs a woman that is too controlling or too much of a feminist either.

We want our men to compromise with us. We want our opinion to have weight and value in our relationships. We want to be our man's equal; his better half. But no real woman should want a man that is a push over either.

A lot of us sistahs are guilty of the same crime once we land the men that we love: we try to change him. A man that once said "no" to certain things is now expected to say "yes dear" just to avoid confrontation with you. A man that hung out with his boys every Friday for poker night now needs your permission to leave the house. You might think you have your man under your control or "pussy whipped" but all you're doing is emasculating him. That's not how you treat a man. Remember that men are problem solvers and want their input respected. They want their manhood respected. A real man, especially the alpha males out there, will always want to tell you how to spend and budget money, how to drive a car, how to clean the house, how to cook his meals, how he wants his children raised, even how to ride his dick. And usually he's right about those things. So let your man be a man.

Men are not known for sharing their feelings. They think more than they speak. And once they make a decision, it's made. If your man is speaking up about certain issues at home or in your relationship it's because he loves you and wants to make things work. He's trying to balance things out before he walks out. That's what real men do. A man that doesn't speak doesn't care. I'm proud of all the sistahs out there that are lawyers and doctors; business women and entrepreneurs; educators and administrators. We're doing the damn thing! But our men should be the head our households and kings of our hearts. We must be the strong women walking next to our men instead of the kind trying to push him out of the way. Even when he's wrong or just being stubborn, find ways to show your man that you were both right. It's all about the balance. Remember the balance.

Another fatal mistake we sistahs make is changing from who we were when we met our men. Brothers often complain, "She used to be my best friend; she used to be cool; she used to be fun". Now your more like his enemy or warden; you're cold instead of cool; and a bore instead of the fun loving girl he met. Drastic personality changes scare a man off. It's almost like you were pretending to be someone else just to land him. Now he doesn't know who you are? If you're even the same woman he fell in love with or was it all a façade? Forget about the sistahs that totally change personalities when a title is involved. When they become a man's "fiancé" or "wife" they start acting more like his "mother" or a "dictator". No Buena mama. No good.

Remember that everything in the dark will eventually come to light. So always be true to yourself and be true to your man.

Chapter 10

How to Love a Black Man when…He's the Real Deal

"Do the right thing."-Spike Lee

So we've discussed the mama's boys and the players, the users and the abusers. We all know how bad a black man can be and how difficult it is to have a relationship with a brother going through these "bad boy" phases. But now I want to focus on the real brothers out there: The brothers that hold us down. The brothers that love us despite our flaws and treat us like queens. The brothers that put family right after God on their list of life's priorities. The brothers that go to work every day. The brothers that support and raise their children. The brothers that don't mind picking up a check or opening your door for you. The real deal.

As much as we complain about there being a shortage of good black men in this world, we must first examine what our definition of a good black man is. For a lot of sistahs a good man looks a certain way, drives a certain car, and makes a certain amount of money. They have a checklist for their "perfect man". So if a brother doesn't have a six pack, drive a Mercedes, and make six figures, he has no chance.

Sistahs that choose men based on these factors are once again following the Western protocol for love and relationships. It's kind of like the movies that come out of Hollywood studios every day. You meet your definition of the "perfect guy"; you have perfect dates with flowers and candy; you have perfect sex; then suddenly you're in love. Then your "perfect guy" buys you get the perfect ring; you have the perfect wedding; and seven years later you get divorced and start all over again. If that sounds like the perfect ending to you, continue to pick men based on this protocol. But if you're looking for spiritual love; the kind of the love that grows; the kind that endures, you better start looking a little deeper than a "perfect guy" checklist.

For one thing there are no perfect people walking this earth. You can be the most handsome man or beautiful woman; you can be rich, be in great shape, even get plastic surgery; but all those things won't make you perfect. If all it took to find love was aesthetic perfection, why do women like Halle Berry have a difficult time finding love? Why are Eva Longoria and Tony Parker and countless other celebrity couples getting divorced every year? There are no perfect people in this world, but I do believe there is someone perfect for everyone.

Good black men come in different packages. A good man may not be making six figures now, but he's responsible with his money; works hard every day; puts in overtime when he needs too; and is looking toward the future. Even if you're making more money than he does now, so what? More money means a better life for both of you regardless of who makes it. What difference does it make who makes more money if you're together for better or worse, richer or poorer, in sickness and in health, 'til death do you part? Is money more important than having a loving husband; a good father for your children; and a partner in life? Money only seems to matter when it's time to divide things up in divorce court. So if your man has to have lots of cash and a stack of credit cards to keep you, it's all good. I just hope that's not all he has going for himself.

A good black man may not have rippling muscles and time to hit the gym every day, but he still looks great in a suit and even better in his boxers. He can chase the kids around the yard and still chase you around the bedroom. If a man loves you and loves his life, you can encourage him to develop better eating habits and get into better shape. If you hit the gym, he will too. Discrediting every man that doesn't have a six pack can't be the way to find true love. As far as I remember from my days at the gym, lots of people meet and date there, but don't necessarily find true love. Bigger muscles don't always equal a bigger heart. And for all ya'll that don't know about Big Poppa, there's nothing like cuddling up on his warm belly on a cold winter's night. There's a lot of pushing in that cushion, so don't count the overweight lovers out.

◊

When you have the real deal, a real man in your life, love is easy. Things happen naturally. This brother is done playing games. He's done playing the field. He's not dogging you out or breaking your heart. He's investing in your relationship and planning for the future. You don't have to pressure this brother to buy you a ring or marry you; he has tears in his eyes the day you approach the altar. And if he's not in the delivery room pushing with you, he's nervously pacing the halls until his child is born. This man loves you. He loves your body. He loves your mind. He loves your spirit. He's your soul mate, your lover, your best friend. He's not perfect but neither are you. Fortunately you guys are perfect for each other.

So how do you love a black man when he's the real deal? When dealing with a man on this level he needs certain things from his woman to make the relationship work. For one thing he needs your unconditional love and understanding. He needs you to be confident in the relationship and have confidence in him. He needs your loyalty and respect. He needs you to be his better half when he's at his worst and his support system when he's at his best. The brother basically needs to be able to trust you with his life. Now those are the biggies; the foundation.

On a day-to-day basis a man's needs are much easier. He may need a little quiet time to read the paper or listen to the news before he asks about your day. He may just need you to fix him a sandwich and hand him the remote without an argument when he misses dinner. Sometimes he may need you to roll over in the middle of the night and give him a little pussy without all the foreplay. Or let him hit it in the morning before he leaves for work. And last, but certainly not least...a man needs his woman to know when to just shut the fuck up so he can think straight. It's really that simple.

Whatever his needs, if you show this man how well you can take care of him and that you want him to be happy, he'll want to take care of you too. A man's happiness is worth a lot to him.

A LOOK IN THE MIRROR

So many times we have the real deal in our lives and don't know it. We sabotage our relationships with our jealousies and insecurities. We can be silly and childish, playing our own little games. We're outright bitchy and moody and push good men away.

There are some other issues I wanted to address about a woman's behavior that effect our relationships with a good man as well:

FRIENDS

Our real friends love us and usually want the best for us. When you meet a man, they are happy and excited about your new prospect. They have lots of tips and advice for you while you're dating and getting to know this man. But once you are in a relationship with this man, especially if you are married to him, when you need advice about your relationship or you're having a problem, talk to him about it first. Communication is the key to a successful relationship. Only the two of you can resolve your differences. A lot of times we just want our friends to support us and to let us vent our frustrations. What we end up getting is a lot of subjective advice from someone who is as emotionally involved as we are. They feel hurt and frustrated by the situation too. If we hate him, they hate him. If we're crying, they're crying. Our friends will always be on our side. It would be better to talk with your pastor or see a couple's therapist to you get a more objective opinion about your situation if you two can't work it out on your own.

Another problem with getting advice about your man from your friend is a lot of times your friends are not in happy relationships of their own. They've been hurt by men and are in full male-bashing mode when you call them upset about something you're man did. They may be angry and bitter about their own failed relationships and are the first ones to tell you, "leave him; he ain't shit; you deserve better". They may be right, but we really need to come to that realization on our own before we break up our relationships and homes.

I also want you to keep in mind that some women just love drama. They don't have a clue what a happy and peaceful relationship looks like because all their relationships are filled with drama. Your relationship becomes their favorite reality show and they feed off the negativity. You have to know when to change the channel with friends like that.

In traditional Afrikan societies, when a couple is to be married, a dowry is paid for the bride. Some people may find this practice archaic and offensive, suggesting a man is buying his wife, but that's not what the dowry system is all about. A dowry gets both sides of the family involved in the marriage. The marriage is discussed and approved by the people that love you guys the most; people that are invested in your future. When you call your mother or in-laws complaining about your husband, instead of saying, "leave him, he ain't shit", they will let you vent your feelings, then advise you on how to work things out between you and your man. For one thing, they know in the event of a divorce your family will have to pay the dowry back and for two, your mother or elder family member knows the difference between a serious matter and a trivial one. Your marriage grows deeper with each obstacle you overcome. It's a shame African-American families don't follow such a beneficial tradition.

Relationships are not easy. It takes effort and compromise to make them work. If you're not getting relationship advice from a professional or someone in a stable relationship, be careful about who you discuss the details of your situation with. Your friend is your friend, but your man is your man. No one will see your man's dirty draws if you don't air it in the front yard.

PMS

Every month we all get a visit from Mother Nature AKA "Aunt Flow", the curse, your period, your menses, your cycle, etc. Whatever you call your "time of the month", I think we all agree it sucks. We feel tired, achy, and bloated. We get terrible cramps and pimples all over our faces. What we need to keep in mind is that it not only sucks for us, it sucks for our men too.

Of course our men don't experience our physical symptoms, but they do experience the emotional ones. We're moody, irritable, anxious, overly sensitive, and just plain bitchy towards them. Our men don't know if or how they can help. The irony of the situation is if a man dare blame the changes in your emotional behavior on your period, it's Hurricane Katrina all over again. He will surely find himself in the eye of the storm with his only chance of survival to hide in the basement until it passes. But it doesn't have to be that way.

PMS or any changes in our emotional and physical health prior to the start of our menses is a predictable event. It shouldn't be an unexpected natural disaster for you or your man. There's no need to wonder why we feel or behave in a certain way for the weeks before our flow starts because we can control the situation. Stress, excess sugar and caffeine, too much sodium and low levels of certain vitamins and minerals in our diets; and a lack of exercise all contribute to how bad our PMS will be or whether we have to experience PMS at all.

Our menstrual cycles signal a fresh start for our reproductive systems. It's a reminder of our ability to produce and sustain life. It's also a time of cleansing for our bodies. How much cleansing the body has to do is up to you? If you sit around filling your body with junk food every day, when that "time of the month" comes, your body has to work harder to do its job causing havoc on your emotional and physical well-being. Having our periods is no excuse for getting crazy once a month. It is our responsibility as women to take care of our bodies by eating more fruits, vegetables, and whole grain foods; exercising and taking our vitamins; decreasing our alcohol intake; quit smoking; and finding positive ways of dealing with our stress like taking a yoga class or relaxing with friends. There are also certain herbal teas we should drink throughout the month like red raspberry leaf, chamomile, and black cohosh that help to clean and detoxify our reproductive organs. Don't get me wrong, I love my sweets and exercise has become a daily battle between me and laziness; but I try to balance things out.

So take care of yourself sistahs. Everything in moderation will help you feel and look better in the long run. Remember, your man shouldn't be the only one watching your figure.

RATIONING IT OUT

I was surprised to discover that many women use a tactic call "rationing it out" when it comes to having sex with their man. I guess I'm just a little different from these women because when it comes to sex, I can be just like a man. I don't care how mad we are at each other or how busy I am; we can go back to being mad after my orgasm. But these women that are "rationing it out" actually withhold sex whenever they are mad at their men; or they use sex to influence their men to do or give them something they want.

Any man with a brain knows if he really messed up and his woman is pissed off about something he should probably just leave her alone for the night; let things cool off. And the doctor makes it clear there is no sex for six weeks after you have a baby unless you want another one right away. But other than those two reasons what sense does it make to withhold sex from a man? Men think about sex a million times a day. Sexual images are everywhere and used in almost every advertisement geared towards men. The ratio of women to men in this country is at least 2:1 not counting the brothers in jail and the ones that are gay. Let us not forget the white girls ready to scoop our men up. So while you're busy "rationing it out", don't forget how easy your man can get it somewhere else.

Sometimes the sistahs "rationing it out" aren't even mad at their men; their telling their men they are "too tired" or "have a headache tonight". We all have days when we may not feel a 100%. But unless you have cancer or some other debilitating illness, you can't be giving your man the same tired excuses over and over. I'm shocked when I hear women say they haven't had sex with their men for months, years even; that they don't buy lingerie anymore. Exactly how long do you expect a man to go without sex? A disciplined man may go a few weeks. But after that it's a wrap. 'Cause if there's anything a man likes better than pussy, it's new pussy. So you better find ways to keep yours new and exciting for him. Why do you think stores like Victoria Secrets, La Perla, and Fredrick's exist? Why does every department store have a lingerie department? Why are there sex shops and strip clubs all over the world? Men are sexual creatures. Men love the visual. It's your duty to keep things interesting in the bedroom for the both of you.

If you have a headache, nothing relieves a headache like an orgasm. If you're not having them, you need to talk to your man about it and try some new things. Orgasms release the tension in your body and relax you. Why do you think boxers abstain from sex before a big fight? They need that tension in their bodies to knock another man out. You don't! If you're tired take a quick shower and eat something sweet to perk yourself up. And if you already took a shower and feel too lazy to get out of bed again have lazy sex. There are side lying positions that use minimal exertion on your part, but still allow your man to get his nut off. You did your job, he's happy, and you both go to sleep feeling good.

And why aren't you having sex with your man anyway? We're supposed to be showing our men how great monogamy is and when they finally commit to it we starve them of the best part! If I was your man and you continuously turned me down for sex, you know what I would be thinking-that you're having sex with someone else. Then I would start thinking about all the women I pass up on a daily basis and get right back out there in the game.

Remember ladies, a man is going to be a man. Even the good ones can slip up from time to time, especially when they are not getting any affection or attention at home. So if your man is still hot for you after 10 years and a couple of kids, he's a keeper. Do whatever it takes to keep those fires burning.

FREE MILK

So you have the real deal. Things are great between you guys. You're ready, been ready, to take the next step in your relationship. You live together. You have a child together. You're beyond playing house and want to make things official. You want the ring, the wedding, the last name, the whole shebang. You want to get married but he still hasn't asked you and you can't understand why.

The problem here is as old as the adage-"Why buy the cow when you can get the milk for free?"

I don't know anyone who doesn't like to get a deal or discount on something valuable. We all love a sale. So if your man already has the house, the "wife", and the kids without having to buy an expensive ring; pay for a wedding; or legally give up his freedom; why would he want to get married? Why should he now pay for something he's been getting for free?

How many women actually prefer moving in their man over getting married or engaged? Moving in with each other is usually a man's brilliant answer to "where is this relationship going?" It's like a consolation prize. He's willing to make you his roommate, but he's not willing to make you his wife. That's not really what you want. But like parents that spoil their kids you say yes just to make him happy; to make yourself seem more pleasing; more desirable. Sorry to say ladies giving in to your man's every wish does not make you desirable. Desire is anticipation. Desire is making a man want more of you. It's our responsibility to keep our men wanting more. He should be dying to put a ringer on your finger; he should be hoping and praying you'll say yes. That's what desire is all about.

Let your man be the fisherman and you the catch. Let him wait patiently on you. Remember you're the prize. Men get a thrill out of reeling in the big catch. Moving in with a man without a commitment of marriage is like a fish jumping on the boat and saying "here I am, don't bother to throw out the line and waste your bait, just clean me up and eat me now". Where's the thrill in that? Remember men love sports; they love the hunt. You'll mean more to him if he has to put in a little work to get you.

Another thing you have to realize about moving in with each other is, your place was your place and his place was his. But once you share a home with a man, he's going to expect you to be a homemaker. Sure he might still take out the trash and mow the lawn. But you will definitely find yourself cooking more, cleaning more, and performing other duties similar to a wife. Trust and believe that while you guys are just "living together" he will be paying attention to whether you are "wife" material. A man will always be pleased to find his mama or Martha Stewart in the kitchen. But if you're not, he can use your lack of domestic skills as an excuse not to marry you later on.

Your sex life changes when you move in together as well. Before you guys moved in with each other your man had to get up, get dressed, and make a trip to your house if he wanted to get some. Now all he has to do is roll over and there the pussy is-more free milk. Next thing you know you're pregnant.

Even if you have children together, that doesn't mean you should automatically move in with each other. Any normal man should want to build his family and home. Family is the cornerstone of society. Keep letting him come by your place, walk through the front door, and feel what he's missing out on. Let him smell home cooking before he even turns the key; let him feel the joy of his son running to greet him before he even crosses the threshold; let him kiss his daughter good night while she's sleeping in her little princess bed. He'll figure out where he belongs. He will want to be with his family. Real men want families. They want that security. If being separated from his family doesn't make him step up, he never will, and you need to move on. There are plenty of good brothers out there that will fit right into the family you created.

And as for the whole "getting to know each other better" theory; isn't that what dating is for? While you're dating a man and you discover his place smells like a boys' locker room and there's nothing but a bed, flat screen TV, and X-Box there, that's who he is. He lives in a "man-cave" and is most likely waiting for the right woman to come along and add that feminine touch to his life. Furthermore he may still have some growing up to do if he still plays with video games. If however you're man likes the finer things in life; has artwork, a nice décor, and appears as though his mama taught him how to clean up after himself; that's who he is. I doubt he'll surprise you and become a slob if you move in together. Same goes for you. If you keep a home fit for a queen, you'll keep a home fit for a king when you guys do get married. If however, your sink is always filled with dirty dishes and you've had the same sheets on your bed for 3 weeks, that's not going to change just because your man moves in. Obviously that's who you are and that's probably why you don't have a man ready to marry you now. You're not prepared for love or a committed relationship if you can't even keep your house clean. What more is there for him to know?

If you and your man are not engaged or actively planning to get married, it's not a good idea to start acting like you are. Keep your own apartment. You don't need to live with each other and you don't have to start a family with him yet. Use birth control until you're sure he's really "the one"-meaning truly committed to sharing his life with you; truly committed to having and building a family with you; and seriously planning for your future together. If a man doesn't know after 3-4 years of dating that he wants to marry you, you may not be "the one" for him. He may not be the one for you.

I know a guy that's been with his girl for fourteen years. They've been living together, no kids, no ring. He finally proposed to her this year. But guess what? He didn't propose because he's ready to get married. He only bought her the ring because she threatened to leave him. My advice to this sistah is be prepared for a lengthy engagement girlfriend. That's the problem with the free milk syndrome. Just like "Massa" didn't want to give up his slaves and all that free labor; why would a man give up his free supply of milk?

◊

Another reason couples move in with each other before getting married or engaged is for financial and economic reasons.

With gas prices, cost of living expenses, and unemployment rates increasing in this country every day, of course it makes sense to move in with your man if you're spending the majority of your time at his place or him at yours. You can split the expenses and chores 50-50, making life easier for the both of you. The problem is things aren't going to stay 50-50 for long. Sure as long as you both stay employed you will continue to split the bills. But suppose one of you gets fired or laid off. Can your salary support you both? Can his? A situation like that can put a terrible strain on your relationship. Financial difficulties are the number one cause of divorce in this country. Are you guys committed to each other on that level without being married? Isn't that commitment worth him giving you his last name? If you had a roommate that couldn't keep up on the bills, you would find a new roommate right? Are you ready to find a new man if things get tough?

◊

So to all my sistahs out there, if you have a good man in your life, don't mess him up by confusing things. A man has a hard enough time trying to navigate and conquer the world out there; especially the brothers. Keep shit real simple for him when it comes to his personal life. If you're dating, date. He can see other people and so can you. If you're committed, be committed, and build on your relationship together.

And when problems arise, keep the lines of communication open. Communication is the key to any healthy relationship. And most importantly, no free milk. He got free milk from his mama. Let him pay for yours.

THE ALTERNATIVES

So what are the alternatives to finding and sticking with a good brother? We discussed the explosion of homosexuality in the black community earlier in the book. If you choose to live your life as a lesbian and that's your thing, God Bless you.

The other big alternative I've been hearing about for sistahs is to date outside of our race. They say a lot of sistahs don't date outside their race and that's why so many of us are single. First let me say, you never hear about white people pushing their daughters to date outside their race. If it happens, they accept it. But I'm sure little Sarah is not encouraged to marry Mandingo over Jim Bob. Secondly, if we're talking about sistahs dating white men, no white man will ever turn down a sistah that is interested in him. White men have wanted us since plantation days. They actually use to tell their wives that the new generations of slaves were born lighter skinned because of a scientific process called symbiosis, not because they were lusting after and raping us. They couldn't admit how attracted they were to the same black women they considered "animals". So trust and believe white men are proud to make us their wives now; delighted to produce children that don't have to tan to have some color.

As for the brothers whom go after white women, like it or not, that also goes back to plantation days as well. White women have been lusting for the brothers since way back then too. Countless brothers were lynched for supposedly even looking at white women, when really it was the white women looking at them. Newspaper headlines read, "Protect white womanhood from the crazy niggers" as though white women needed more protection than the sistahs did. We were the ones getting raped. We were the ones whose babies were stolen in the middle of the night. We were the ones being sold on the auction block and separated from our families. White women have always been prized possessions placed on a protective pedestal by the white man. It's sad to see my own brothers now protecting them instead of us. For some reason brothers have this idea that white women are easier to deal with than the sistahs; forgetting what sistahs have been through; forgetting what many of them have put sistahs through; forgetting a sistah will be with his ass even when he's dead broke. The other day on Good Morning America they had a story about a brother proposing to a white woman on a TV commercial he made because he felt the ring he bought wasn't "good enough" for her. Do you think that same brother would do that for his own sistah? Doubt it.

Don't get me wrong, I understand "you can't help who you fall in love with". I've heard it many times. What I don't understand is why some brothers and sistahs exclude each other as potential options for love. Why do we put ourselves in a position to fall only for "the alternatives"? A cousin of mine informed me that many internet dating sites have brothers listing their preference as "sisters need not apply". And I know many sistahs that surround themselves with white friends in a white world further increasing the probability of dating and falling in love with a white man.

White men will always love the sistahs and white women will always love the brothers. And if you didn't know by now, most white people are totally mesmerized by the dark skin of a black people. I have had many white people tell me I have beautiful skin. I have had many white people ask me if they could touch my hair. Yet to my own brothers and sistahs my hair may be too nappy, my skin too dark. Many brothers are still caught up on light skin and long hair as their only definition of beauty. As a whole, we all seem to be fascinated by interracial or mixed people as though it's the other race in them that makes them beautiful; not the black part. Many of us are still ashamed of our roots. We call each other "blacky; nappy; niggah; midnight; tar baby; pickaninny; black bitch; etc." because that's what we were taught. We were taught to hate each other. We were taught to hate ourselves.

Imagine if we made an effort to say "my brother; my sister; my king; or my queen" when referring to our own people. What a difference it would make in our interactions with each other as brothers and sisters. What a difference it would make in our relationships and self-image.

So while you're busy considering all the alternatives out there, just be sure you know why you really need one.

Chapter 11

A Look in the Mirror

Well my sistahs, it's been real. I greeted you with ancient peace and love and I'm leaving you on that note. We talked a lot about our men, why they do the things they do, and how to love them despite it all. But I think the most important thing we did, something I hadn't planned when I started writing this book, was to take a look at ourselves: a look in the mirror.

I believe in change. I believe we can change ourselves. I believe we can change our circumstances. I believe we can change our world. But while we're waiting for that change to happen, always remember the only factor you can control in life, the only behaviors you can effectively change, are your own. We can't make our men be committed if they're not ready. We can't make them be faithful, loyal, or more responsible when they're stuck in those negative phases. We can't make them love us. I've seen and felt the pain of loving a black man through those times and believe me when I say not only was it heartbreaking, it almost destroyed my soul.

It was at those times I decided to focus more on myself. I took time to heal. Time to love myself and be the example of the kind of love I wanted in my life. I spent more time in prayer and meditation; more time exercising and strengthening my body; and put more effort into furthering my education and career. I also spent more time surrounded by the people I knew loved me, like my family and friends; and less time chasing these men. If the brothers keep breaking your heart; keep letting you down; keep starving you of the love and happiness you deserve, I suggest you do the same.

When we love ourselves, love will come. Let love come to you. That's the power of love. That's the power of a black woman. And that's how to love a black man when…

I thank you for your love and support and hope my words inspire change and love amongst our people. Feel free to contact me at howtoloveablackmanwhen@gmail.com or on Facebook with any questions or comments you might have. I look forward to hearing from you.

Peace.

And

Dedicated to My Brothers: An Awesome Wonder

Image taken from Without Sanctuary:Lynching

Photography in America

Twin Palms Publishers 2000

An Awesome Wonder

*The Black Man has been an awesome wonder
since the beginning of time.*

Fearless and strong in his youth,

majestic in his prime.

When whips and chains could not break his spirit,

they started on his mind.

Run nigger, dumb nigger,

leave your family behind.

Drink my liquor,

use my drugs.

Live in my cage,

be a thug.

*The Black Man has been an awesome wonder
since the beginning of time.*

Feared for his nature,

loved for his design.

When poverty could not break his spirit,

they started on his gifts.

Sing nigger, dance nigger,

give my bank account a lift.

Work for my company,

play for my team.

Sing for my label,

it's the American dream.

*The Black Man has been an awesome wonder
since the beginning of time.*

My lover, my friend, truly one of a kind

-sistahsophie